*Literature
for Young People
on War and Peace*

Recent Titles in
Bibliographies and Indexes in World Literature

LITERATURE FOR YOUNG PEOPLE ON WAR AND PEACE

An Annotated Bibliography

Compiled by
HARRY EISS

Bibliographies and Indexes in World Literature,
Number 24

GREENWOOD PRESS
New York • Westport, Connecticut • London

Library of Congress Cataloging-in-Publication Data

Eiss, Harry Edwin.
  Literature for young people on war and peace : an annotated
bibliography / compiled by Harry Eiss.
    p. cm. — (Bibliographies and indexes in world literature,
ISSN 0742-6801 ; no. 24)
    ISBN 0-313-26068-0 (lib. bdg. : alk. paper)
    1. Young adult literature—Bibliography. 2. Bibliography—Best
books—Young adult literature. 3. War in literature—Bibliography.
4. Peace in literature—Bibliography. I. Title. II. Series.
Z1037.E38   1989
[PN1009.A1]
016.8088'0358'0835—dc20   89-17212

British Library Cataloguing in Publication Data is available.

Library of Congress Catalog Card Number: 89-17212
ISBN: 0-313-26068-0
ISSN: 0742-6801

First published in 1989

Greenwood Press, Inc.
88 Post Road West, Westport, Connecticut 06881

Printed in the United States of America

The paper used in this book complies with the
Permanent Paper Standard issued by the National
Information Standards Organization (Z39.48-1984).

10 9 8 7 6 5 4 3 2 1

For my children,
Meghan, Israel, Angela, Jared, and Ryan;
and for all of the children throughout the world,
may they live in peace

Contents

Preface

Pablo Picasso claimed that art is the lie that lets us
see the truth. If this is true, then there must be something
about art (of which fiction is a subgenre) that separates it
from other forms of expression. That it is a lie seems self-
evident (at least it is not necessary here to go into philosophical arguments over whether the illusions of fiction are
literally true). What is more important is how fiction can
reveal or, in a certain sense, be truth.

An inquiry into the truth in fiction leads directly into
the theories of the Romantic Movement, when a great deal of
time was spent trying to distinguish between reason and
imagination. John Keats, for instance, argued strongly that
"what the imagination seizes as Beauty must be truth"
("Letters," Nov. 22, 1817).

This separation of truth from reason can, perhaps, be
most easily understood within contemporary left/right brain
theory. According to this theory, the left side of the brain
thinks in a rational, logical, and sequential manner, the
manner generally given to the term reason, and the manner
generally employed to explain reality.

The right side of the brain, however, works in a spon-
taneous, wholistic, intuitive manner (the form of dream),
and, rather than explaining reality, understands and expresses
reality in symbols. Symbols, similes, metaphors--these are
not literally true, but figuratively true. Here is the key.
A work of fiction is not literally true (it is a lie), but it
carries a symbolic truth. Thus, art is the literal lie that
reveals the figurative truth.

Of what value is figurative truth? Some truths, the most
important truths, cannot be explained in the left brain manner
of rational thinking. If they could, then humans would be
nothing more than complex combinations of chemicals. There
would be no such thing as spirit or soul. Sadness would be
nothing more than a condition caused by the build up or
combination of certain chemicals, as would love, hate,
laughter, and all of the human emotions. There would be no
need for any of the concerns that now fall under the term
ethos. Good and bad, right and wrong, just and unjust--these
terms would have no more meaning for humans than they now do
for the motions of the oceans.

However, at least at present, such human emotions are not
reduced to explanation. And it might be mentioned that the
explanations of science, mathematics, and philosophy do not
give any more provable answers to such questions as creation
than do the stories--the expressions of fiction.

To put it all into a framework--mythos (fiction)
expresses the ethos (values) of a culture. Here is where the

meaning of life is to be related and understood. If fiction,
then, provides expressions of the meaning of life, it is the
lie that reveals the truth.

Furthermore, the greatest truths of the human condition
are revealed under the most strenuous of conditions, such as
those to be found during a war. Literature dealing with war,
then, will offer expressions of the most important truths
of the human condition.

The question then becomes one of determining when a
human, a child, is capable of understanding and handling
these truths. Consider the following: A soldier from one
large country stands on a long wall. He holds a bomb powerful
enough to blow up the entire world in his hand. A soldier
from another large country also stands on the wall. He too
holds a bomb powerful enough to blow up the entire world.
Most of the other people in both countries are in bomb
shelters. The book ends.

This scenario sounds like a book for adults about the
cold war and the build up of nuclear weapons by the United
States and the Soviet Union. It isn't. It's a picture book
by Dr. Seuss, and it's done in the same rhythmic style as all
his other picture books for children. Many libraries stock it
in the adult book sections.

Highly respected children's picture book author and
illustrator, Raymond Briggs created WHEN THE WIND BLOWS (020),
a cartoon style picture book intended for adults about a
bumbling older couple who stumble about, trying to recite some
Bible passages before their imminent deaths from the nuclear
apocalypse. He wrote and illustrated it for adults; however,
it was a popular book on the children's sales charts.

The highly acclaimed artist Toshi Maruki wrote and
illustrated HIROSHIMA NO PIKA (207), a graphic picture book
about the bombing of Hiroshima, filled with pictures and
discussions of the dying and dead, in the hope that informing
young people might help prevent it ever happening again.

Roberto Innocenti created ROSE BLANCHE (165), a
beautifully done picture book about the taking of the Jews to
concentration camps during World War II. The ending of the
story implies that the young girl who witnessed this was
accidentally killed.

Although these books may not form the center of children's
literature, they do represent an important portion of it,
revealing some tragic and yet often wonderous truths about the
human condition and how noble humans are capable of acting
under extreme hardships.

These are the types of books this bibliography
discusses--books aimed at children about war and peace. Such
books, since they deal with eternal aspects of the human
condition, are themselves, as is all good fiction, eternal.
However, they have extra significance during this time of
world tension and real possibility of nuclear holocaust.
Although the literal accuracy of the following statistics
rapidly becomes dated, they do represent the general trends
and overall world condition of recent years.

According to a survey in the NEW ENGLAND JOURNAL OF
MEDICINE ("American and Soviet Teenager's Concerns about
Nuclear War and the Future," Vol. 319, No. 7, Aug 26, 1988,
pp. 407-413), conducted by Eric Chivian, M.D.; John P.
Robinson, Ph.D., Jonathan R.H. Tudge, Ph.D., Nikolai P. Popov,
D.Sci., and Vladimir G. Andreyenkov, Ph.D., American youths
rank fear of nuclear war as their second highest worry (only

the fear of a parent dying is greater); 42% think there will
be a nuclear war in their lifetime; Soviet youths rank fear of
a nuclear war as their greatest worry.

Today's children have lived their entire lives under the
threat of immediate annihilation through nuclear holocaust.
The arms race of the cold war is on the news almost every
night, and it affects every aspect of their lifes, from the
declining position of the United States in the world's economy
to their plans for a future (or lack of one).

Here are some facts: During a span of six years,
50 million people were killed in World War II. The combined
firepower, including the two atomic bombs dropped on Japan,
equalled three million tons of TNT--three megatons. Any one
Poseidon submarine has over 200 warheads aboard with a
firepower capability of nine megatons--three times the
firepower expended in World War II. Any one Poseidon
submarine could destroy all the large and medium-sized cities
in the Soviet Union.

Scientists have computed that the explosion of only 1%
of the arsenals of the United States and the Soviet Union
would sufficiently darken the skies to cause the temperature
to drop to 20 degrees below zero for months and destroy all
plant life in the northern hemisphere. In addition, burning
cities and plastics would cause toxic gases. Radioactive
particles would be widespread. Plants, animals, and humans
surviving the initial explosions would die from a multitude of
causes--frost, famine, radiation, pollution.

According to Joshua Handler and William M. Arkin, NUCLEAR
WARSHIPS AND NAVAL NUCLEAR WEAPONS: A COMPLETE INVENTORY
(Washington, D.C.: Greenpeace and the Institute for Policy
Studies, May, 1988), as of May 1988, the navies of the United
States, the Soviet Union, the United Kingdom, France, and
China made up 30% of the total world arsenal of nuclear
weapons. As of December 1987, their combined number of ships
and submarines equalled 1,101, and their aircraft carriers
equalled 3,250. Their fleets carried 1,792 submarine-launched
ballistic missiles (SLBMs) armed with 9,487 nuclear warheads
(each with an explosive power from 1 to 1,000 kilotons), an
estimated 6,400 non-strategic nuclear warheads (mainly
antisubmarine warfare (ASW) weapons), 1,950 aircrafts with
nearly 2,000 nuclear weapons, approximately 550 nuclear
sea-launched cruise missiles (SLCMs) (a number expected to
increase rapidly), and some 550 surface-to-air missiles
(SAMs); in addition, the Soviet Union deployed some 200
warheads on ten ships.

All told, these navies have 16,071 nuclear weapons (only
slightly less than 1/3 of the total world arsenal). These
weapons can fire multiple warheads, varying in explosive
power. The least powerful warhead, 1 kiloton, equals 1/30 of
the total explosive power of World War II; the most powerful
equals 10 times the total explosive power of World War II; and
the standard warhead on the Poseidon C3 missile, which carries
six to fourteen such warheads, equals 40 kilotons.

If nothing else, it should be apparent that there are
currently enough nuclear weapons in existence to destroy the
earth several times over. Whether this power is good or bad
or bad-but-necessary, and so on, is not the point
here--rather, the point is that it is the reality under which
all of today's children have grown-up.

In addition to this real possibility of an instant end to
the human race, consider how the following statistics

influence children's lives (once again, the point is not
whether the actions are right or wrong, only that they are
real. President Reagan's fiscal year 1987 budget was, yet
again, an attempt to dramatically increase spending on
national defense and nuclear weapons, while cutting back on
social programs. The following figures obtained from the
Defense Department indicate the president's proposed budget
allocations for fiscal year 1987 (the figures in parentheses
indicate the percentage difference from the 1986 budget
allocations): Star Wars, $4.8 billion (+74%); Trident II
Missile, $3.1 billion (+10%); MX Missile, $1.8 billion (-27%,
down because of a 1986 cap placed on the program);
Midgetman Missile, $1.4 billion (+124%); Trident Submarine,
$1.7 billion (+17%); Anti-Satellite Weapons, $.3 billion
(+62%); and Tomahawk Cruise Missile, $.9 billion (+9%).
        These huge increases came at a time when the Gramm-
Rudman-Hollings Act, signed into law in 1986, demanded a
reduction of the Fiscal Year 1987 budget from its projected
$170 billion to $144 billion. Yet the proposed Department of
Defense budget was $320.3 billion, an 8.3% increase above
inflation over the 1986 budget. The only ways of off-setting
these descrepencies were to increase taxes, something the
president vowed to fight against, or to decrease funding to
social programs. In his state of the Union address, the
president said he would not reduce spending by "taking from
those in need." Yet his fiscal year 1987 budget called for
reductions in spending for low-income programs by $17 billion,
including reductions in Medicaid ($1.7 billion), Child
Nutrition ($549 million), food stamps ($406 million), and
aid to dependent children ($1.3 billion). All together,
Reagan's budget proposals called for cut backs in domestic
programs of $35.4 billion.
        The meaning is obvious. The administration of the
United States under Ronald Reagan saw its major responsibility
as providing a strong military, centered on the development
and deployment of nuclear weapons. The following trade-offs
are the result of spending for the military as opposed to
spending for civilian needs, and indicate even more clearly
the extent of this commitment. Just 7% of the fiscal spending
on the military from 1981 to 1986 equals $100 billion.
That same amount could have been spent rehabilitating the
U.S. steel industry so that it would once again be the most
efficient in the world. The $34 billion spent on the
navy's F-16 fighter program is equal to what it would cost to
upgrade America's machine-tool stock to bring it to the
average age of Japan's. The $11 billion overrun as of 1981 on
the navy's Aegis-cruiser program could have been used to pay
for a comprehensive effort to produce cars that get 80 to 100
miles per gallon.
        The House Budget Committee supplied the following figures
on the president's fiscal year 1987 budget allocations for a
number of domestic programs (once again, the figures in
parentheses indicate the percentage difference from the 1986
budget allocations): subsidized housing, $3.0 billion (-77%);
mass transit, $1.2 billion (-67%); federal crop insurance,
$.24 billion (-33%); job training, $2.9 billion (-17%);
guaranteed student loans, $2.3 billion (-30%); and vocational
adult education, $.5 billion (-47%).
        The Reagan administration rapidly shifted budget
allocations from domestic programs to national defense. Why?
According to SOVIET MILITARY POWER (382), 1986, a publication

put out each year since 1981 by the Defense Department, "The
United States, together with our allies and friends, must
maintain the military capabilities required to deter and, if
necessary, defeat Soviet aggression against our vital
interests" (pp. 156). COUNTERFORCE ISSUES FOR THE U.S.
STRATEGIC NUCLEAR FORCES, put out by the Congressional Budget
Office, January, 1978, estimated that Soviet Nuclear forces in
1985 would consist of the following: 2,438 to 2,688 total
launchers; 8,294 to 8,794 total warheads; 10,111 to 10,211
total megatons. According to the same study, in order to
"maintain the military capabilities required to deter and,
if necessary," defeat Soviet aggression against our vital
interests," the United States would need to have the following
nuclear forces as of 1985: 2,180 total launchers, 13,904
total warheads, and 3,332.5 to 3,629.5 total megatons.
     Both the United States and the Soviet Union have nuclear
arsenals capable of destroying the entire earth many times
over. Even given the argument that the build-up of nuclear
weapons prevents nuclear war, it has to be admitted that the
build-up exacts a tremendous cost, both in terms of economics
(as the above figures amply demonstrate), and, perhaps even
more importantly, in terms of psychological affects of knowing
that at any instant the entire human race might be
annihilated. Robert Jay Lifton, INDEFENSIBLE WEAPONS: THE
POLITICAL AND PSYCHOLOGICAL CASE AGAINST NUCLEARISM (375),
states the following:
          We are just now beginning to realize that nuclear
          weapons radically alter our existence. It is true
          that none of our actions, problems, or symptoms is
          caused by nuclear weapons alone. But it is also
          true that nothing we do or feel--in working,
          playing, and loving, and in our private, family,
          and public lives--is free of their influence. The
          threat they pose has become the context for our
          lives, a shadow that persistently intrudes upon
          our mental ecology. (p. 3)
     Today's children have this omnipresent shadow hanging
over them. It is hard to believe when adults (perhaps
hoping beyond hope) say that children are unaware of war.
WATERMELONS NOT WAR: A SUPPORT BOOK FOR PARENTING IN THE
NUCLEAR AGE (360), just one of many sources of such excerpts,
includes many samples of children talking and writing about
war. Most of the children either questioned the logic
of war or indicated dispair over its prevention, and
though they are representative of what many American
children feel, they seem mild and innocent, when compared
with the reality many children around the world face. In
an article titled "Children and War" by Neil Boothby
(published in CULTURAL SURVIVAL QUARTERLY, Vol. 10, No. 4,
1986), some of the harsher realities children face are
indicated. For example, in Colombia,
          Leon Carlos discovered that
          boys were sometimes forced to kill other children
          of similar ages in order to save their own lives
          and enter into paramilitary groups, acts most
          undertook only after severe beatings ("Unusual
          Patterns of Crime During La Violencia in Colombia,"
          AMERICAN JOURNAL OF PSYCHIATRY, 125: 11 May 1969).
     In a personal interview Neil Boothby recorded in the
same article a 24-year-old Mayan Indian mother description of
the deaths of seven children in her village:

At first we didn't think there would be trouble
because a few days before another group of
soldiers had questioned about giving food to the
guerrillas. When we told them it happened once
and only because the guerrillas had threatened us
they went away. But this time the soldiers said
we had to be punished. They pushed five boys
forward, made them lie face-down on the ground and
shot them in the back. A baby girl was then
pulled from her mother's arms and her skull
crushed against the side of a house. The last
death occurred when a soldier cut open the stomach
of a pregnant woman saying that even our unborns
will not will not [sic] be spared.

Such examples could be multiplied, but the point is made.
It is only necessary to mention the battles taking place in
Israel, Belfast, Nicaragua, Afghanistan, the Persian Gulf, the
recent conflicts in Vietnam and Korea, and the world wars of
not all that long ago, to set the stage. Obviously, war and
conflict, tragic as they are, mold and shape the human
environment (both physical and emotional) at all times, and in
more dramatic and inclusive ways, than any other human
endeavor. This is not to say that, on a personal level, the
death of a parent or some such major tragedy does not affect
children in as great or a greater way--rather, it is to say
that war and conflict are a part of the life of a child, like
it or not.

Therefore, it really is not surprising that a great deal
of the literature for youths concerns the subject of war.
Books for younger children (up to about age seven) often deal
with war (or conflict) in the form of an allegory or parable.
Some of the better ones include: DRUMMER HOFF (087); BANG
BANG YOU'RE DEAD (089); HOW TO TURN WAR INTO PEACE (004); THE
BUTTER BATTLE BOOK (277); THE STORY OF FERDINAND (187); THE
MINSTREL AND THE MOUNTAIN: A TALE OF PEACE (354); and a
version of Mark Twain's THE WAR PRAYER (322), with pictures by
John Groth (which is really for adults and leads to the
following group of picture books).

Some recent well crafted but blunt picture books are
very controversial in terms of the intended audience, among
them: HIROSHIMA NO PIKA (207); ROSE BLANCHE (165); WOLF OF
SHADOWS (294); and WHEN THE WIND BLOWS (020).

In defense of these books as children's literature, it
might be mentioned that Mother Goose rhymes, traditional
folktales, myths, and the Bible, all standard literature for
children, are filled with violence. However, for those who
don't believe that children can gain anything from these harsh
books, there are less realistic books.

These others, often somewhat too simplistically, have
been put out to deal more with conflict and its resolution and
friendship than actual war. Some of the better ones are: THE
HATING BOOK (356); LET'S BE ENEMIES (325); TERRIBLE THINGS
(025); and THE BAD ISLAND (290).

I NEVER SAW ANOTHER BUTTERFLY (329), a collection of
poetry written by children from the Terezin concentration camp
(all of whom were exterminated in Nazi concentration camps)
is, perhaps, the most moving of the books of poetry.

The best biography for younger children comes from Jean
Fritz--nearly all of it concerning famous people of the
American Revolutionary War.

For older youths, the best body of literature (the most

complete group in all the literature on war and peace for
youths) is that dealing with the Jewish Holocaust during World
War II. Good book after good book has been written based on
what happened during that terrible time. Most of them come
from personal experience; many, such as ANNE FRANK: THE DIARY
OF A YOUNG GIRL (104) and YOUNG MOSHE'S DIARY: THE SPIRITUAL
TORMENT OF A JEWISH BOY IN NAZI EUROPE (090), are actual
diaries.
     The American Revolutionary War has been the subject of
many excellent books for all ages, from SAM THE MINUTEMAN
(009), and easy-to-read book, to Ester Forbes' excellent
JOHNNY TREMAIN: A STORY OF BOSTON IN REVOLT (091).
     The American Civil War has also received a great deal of
attention and has been the subject of books for all ages,
including several excellent books about Abraham Lincoln (e.g.,
Carl Sandberg's ABE LINCOLN GROWS UP (272) and Russell
Freeman's LINCOLN: A PHOTOBIOGRAPHY (105)).
     In addition to the excellent books about the Jewish
Holocaust, World War II has several good books on the bombing
of Hiroshima, including such controversial picture books as
HIROSHIMA NO PIKA (164), and such excellent books for older
youth as Hersey's HIROSHIMA (150) and Ibuse's BLACK RAIN
(164).
     Although the line between literature for older youths and
adults is blurry at best, it is, nevertheless, easier to
distinguish in prose than in poetry, and the entries in this
bibliography include a few samples of poetry that most people
would consider adult, e.g., some by Walt Whitman and Stephen
Crane, although generally introduced to secondary school
students.
     Another important category of literature under the rubric
of war and peace is that about pacifists. This literature
should be read in conjunction with the pro-war histories that
are almost standard in the American school system. It
includes such books as AIN'T GONNA STUDY WAR NO MORE: THE
STORY OF AMERICA'S PEACE SEEKERS (212) and MEN AGAINST WAR
(141). Also included in this category are the books about
such people of peace as Martin Luther King, Jr., Gandhi, and
Gladdys Esther Muir. "Civil Disobedience" by Thoreau has been
included, since it serves as such a central work on the
subject, despite it being hard to defend as a book for young
people.
     In addition to the annotated bibliography of materials
for youths, the main focus of this volume, there is an
annotated bibliography on materials for adults about how to
discuss the subject of war and peace with young people.
This somewhat eclectic collection contains everything from war
and peace film guides and bibliographies for further reading
to books about running workshops and staging plays.
     The index to the volume provides access to authors,
illustrators, and titles, subject entries for warriors,
pacifists and other such personalities, categories of certain
types of materials, such as allegories and parables,
and poetry collections.
     Many organizations can be contacted for additional
information on issues of war and peace for both youths and
adults. A computer file containing hundreds of annotated
films on the arms race and nuclear war, periodically updated,
is available by mailing $2 to John Dowling, Physics
Department, Mansfield State College, Mansfield, PA 16933. The
Peace Resource Center: Hiroshima/Nagasaki Memorial Collection,

Pyle Center, Box 1193, Wilmington, OH 45177, puts out a
quarterly newsletter on peace education resources--
audiovisuals, books, posters, and slide sets, rents videos,
and sells books and other materials. Greenpeace USA, 1436 U
Street N.W., Washington, DC 20009, produces similar materials.
The Better World Society, 1140 Connecticut Avenue, N.W., Suite
1006, Washington, DC 20036, has lists of organizations,
speakers, magazines, books, films, and radio programs dealing
with the arms race. Most of the reference materials in the
adult section of this bibliography include lists of sources
for additional materials.

    In 1959 the General Assembly of the League of Nations
adopted the Declaration of the Rights of the Child, affirming
the right of all children to receive special protection,
to be given opportunities and facilities to enable them to
develop in a healthy and normal manner, to enjoy the benefits
of social security (including adequate nutrition, housing,
recreation and medical services), to receive education, and to
be protected against all forms of neglect, cruelty, and
exploitation. The document stresses that "mankind owes to the
child the best it has to give." In a very real sense, our
generation is not living up to that ideal, unless we can
honestly say that our huge expenditures on the weapons of war
are better than a world without hunger--the amount of money
spent in four days on the U.S. national defense could feed the
entire world for a whole year. Keep in mind that "we" does
not refer to any specific nationality, race, or religious
group, but, rather, to all nationalities, all races, and all
religions--the entire human race. After all, we're all in
this together.

    In spite of the cruelty and darkness dealt with by much
of the material in this bibliography, there is, nevertheless,
a strong sense of the beauty and greatness of the human
spirit, which is often best shown when times are black. And,
as many who present such materials to children stress, the
point is not to beat them down with how bad and hopeless life
is, but, rather, to offer hope, to show that, through hard
work, endurance, and courage, humans are capable of overcoming
tremendous hardships. Yes, as Katherine Paterson stated so
well in THE GREAT GILLY HOPKINS, life is hard, but isn't that
after all, what makes it worthwhile--doing a good job at
something that's hard?

    I was on the planning committee for a Montana Committee
for the Humanities sponsored conference, THE CHANGING FACE OF
HUMANITY IN THE NUCLEAR AGE, which discussed "the ways in
which the four decades of the nuclear age have affected our
culture and our collective experience," (Missoula, Montana,
Nov. 6 & 7, 1986). The conference was moderated by Ron Perrin,
Mary Clearman Blew, and Stewart Justman, and featured Robert
Jay Lifton, Christopher Lasch, Robert Bellah, Jean Bethke
Elshtain, Stanley Hauerwas, Dana Boussard, William A.
Kittredge, Stephen Speckart, and Senator William Yellowtail.
I mention this because, during the panel presentations,
William A. Kittredge brought up the need for writers (artists)
to provide stories that resolve the nuclear cold war in a
positive manner. The idea behind positive resolutions is that
humans tend to want to live out stories to their conclusions,
and if the only stories writers are providing have negative
conclusions to the nuclear arms build up, the human race will
feel compelled to live out a nuclear holocaust.

    This idea applies even more strongly to children than to

adults, as children are going through what Jacob Bronowski
calls "the long childhood," a time when they are learning the
ethics of the civilization. The stories children are exposed
to will have a stronger affect on them than stories to which
adults are exposed. Therefore, children need stories that
offer real solutions to real problems (i.e., real solutions to
real war).

This bibliography, then, lists many of the principle
books written for children about the important subject of war
and peace. Several books, though not all, offer possible and
positive solutions to a realistically portrayed negative
situation. Although some of the more important works on
mythic wars, Arthurian romance, and fantasy in general (e.g.,
J.R.R. Tolkien and C.S. Lewis) have been included, this group
of literature as a whole has been left out on the theory
it contains large bodies of literature not central to the
focus of this bibliography and receives a great deal of
attention in other studies.

I want to thank Marilyn Brownstein, Diane Spalding,
Greenwood Press, and the library staff of Eastern Michigan
University.

*Literature
for Young People
on War and Peace*

ANNOTATED BIBLIOGRAPHY

001. Aaron, Chester. GIDEON. Philadelphia: Lippincott, 1982, 181 pp. (ages 11-adult).

Chester Aaron has written a fictionalized autobio-graphical narrative that has been thoroughly researched to provide the feel of authenticity. Gideon, the main character, becomes a member of the resistance in both the Warsaw ghetto and the Treblinka concentration camp, surviving because he is willing to break the law, to deny his identity, and in general, because he refuses to give up. The story is a good presentation of a common theme in the literature of the Holocaust--the human ability to endure.

The book begins with the following quotation from Elizabeth Barrett Browning's "The Cry of the Children":

Do you hear the children weeping, O my
brothers . . .
. . . the young, young children, O my
    brothers,
        They are weeping bitterly!
They are weeping in the playtime of the
others . . .

002. Alcott, Louisa May. HOSPITAL SKETCHES. Redpath, 1863; rpt., New York: Sagamore Press, 1957, 157 pp. (ages 12-18).

Few would not recognize the name of Louisa May Alcott, famous author of LITTLE WOMEN. However, her first popular success (published in the COMMONWEALTH magazine) was this little known work about her experiences as a nurse for the Georgetown Hospital during the Civil War, 1962-1963. She only served for six weeks, contracting typhoid fever and being sent home after that time.

The book is filled with a youthful exuberance and desire to help, and it expresses a naive enthusiasm. In truth it is a love story (John is the love interest, the "manliest man among my forty"), a love that transcends mere physical or individual love to embrace all of humanity.

003. Anderson, Paul L. SWORDS IN THE NORTH. New York: D. Appleton-Century, 1937. 270 pp. (ages 14-adult).

Paul L. Anderson considers Julius Caesar the "strongest personality that has ever lived," and presents this fictional account of what he considers a planned, light invasion into Britain (not meant "for the purpose of conquest") from a thoroughly researched vantage point.

However, a fictional character, Gaius Aemilius Durus,

narrates the story, and the syntax and diction used, apparently in an attempt to add an historic quality to the story, is convoluted and just plain difficult to follow.

004.   Armstrong, Louise. HOW TO TURN WAR INTO PEACE. Illustrated by Bill Basso. New York: Harcourt Brace Jovanovich, 1979, 28 pp. (ages 4-8).

Susie and you (a young boy) are building sand castles on the beach. Since you are right next to each other, "you're in a POTENTIAL TROUBLE SPOT."
The story progresses through the various stages of the build-up and resolution of the conflict using the terminology currently used to describe world conflict, for example:

If Pee Wee comes by and says, "What's up?"--he is a NEUTRAL OBSERVER.
If he offers to NEGOTIATE A SETTLEMENT, this is DIPLOMACY.

The cartoon-style illustrations add humor, at the same time as they capture the personalities of the characters.
This is a fun way to introduce children to the terminology of the cold war, as well as subtly showing the stupidity of combat. It ends with the characters achieving peace.

005.   Arnothy, Christine. I AM FIFTEEN AND I DON'T WANT TO DIE. Trans. from French (anon) New York: Dutton, 1956, 122 pp. (ages 10-adult).

This is an impressionistic autobiographical diary written by a 15-year-old Jewish girl living in Germany during World War II. She is filled with terror, self-pity, and anger-- afraid of both the Nazis and the Russians, constantly worried about death. Her situation was certainly an inhuman one, but her constant whining is irritating.

006.   Baker, Betty. THE DUNDERHEAD WAR. New York: Harper & Row: New York, 1967, 215 pp. (ages 10-14).

Quincy Heffendorf (a year too young to enlist in the Missouri Volunteers) and his Uncle Fritz from Germany latch onto the army as it travels through mud and deserts in pursuit of the Mexican army.

007.   Baker, Betty. THE PIG WAR. Illustrated by Robert Lopshire. New York: Harper & Row, 1969, 64 pp. (ages 5-8).

This is an "I Can Read History" book about an actual war, "The Pig War," that took place on an island off the state of Washington in 1859, where both American and British troops were stationed because neither country knew who the island belonged to. A peaceful rivalry (similar to the one in THE BUTTER BATTLE BOOK by Seuss) becomes a war and is resolved.
The illustrations are simple, cartoon style, and go well with the writing.

008. Baker, Jeffrey J. W. STRIKE THE TENT. Photographs by
Lawrence O. Holmberg, Jr. New York: Doubleday, 1970, 60 pp.
(ages 10-15).

      This book presents the Civil War from the viewpoint of
the South; most directly it is a book about the Army of
Northern Virginia, which, it says, was "one of the greatest
armies that ever marched off to war."
      There are many full color photographs (most of them of
what were once battlefields or are simply pretty foliage of
the South), and the layout is attractive (generally writing on
one page or part of a page and a photograph on the
accompanying page).
      The author makes it a point to emphasize that he is not
attempting to glorify war or the reasons for the Army of
Northern Virginia to fight. However, his attempts to remove
slavery from their reasons comes off lame. Apparently,
according to Baker, the soldiers thought they were fighting
for freedom and liberty (and by extension for the traditional
life style of the South, which the reader cannot help but
realize was based on slavery).
      In other words, STRIKE THE TENT is an interesting attempt
to defend fighting for something (slavery) that it is
generally agreed upon today as wrong by saying that the
soldiers did not know what they were fighting for.
      Unfortunately, there may be a general truth here. How
clearly do soldiers, who bravely march off to kill and die for
their countries, understand the reasons for their dramatic
acts? It is a question worth asking.
      It is hard to place an age on the audience for the book.
The format suggests it is for younger children (large type,
easy-to-read content), but the underlying praise of fighting
(even for a bad cause), unless perceived as irony (which is
certainly not the intent) may make the book unsuited for
children.

009. Benchley, Nathaniel. SAM THE MINUTEMAN. Illustrated by
Arnold Lobel. New York: Harper & Row, 1969, 62 pp. (ages 5-8).

      This is a well written "I Can Read History" book for
beginning readers (large type) about a young boy who fights at
the Battle of Lexington with his father. It realistically
includes the fact that people die in war, but it doesn't dwell
on the details.
      Arnold Lobel's illustrations, expressing a sense of past
time through the use of muted lines, shading and accurate
details, are done in black-and-white with touches of red and
green, and live up to what one would expect from a caldecott
award winning illustrator.

010. Bennett, George and Paul Molloy, ed. CAVALCADE OF POEMS.
New York: Scholastic, 1968, 120 pp. (ages 10-adult).

      This collection of poems is put together in the belief,
taken from Robert Frost, that "no poetry was good enough for
young readers 'that wasn't equally good for their elders.'"
It includes such poems as "The Man He Killed" by Thomas Hardy,
which, in a very simple, straightforward manner, brings war
down to a personal, human level.

011.   Benson, Bernard.   THE PEACE BOOK. London: Cape, 1981.

        This offers an unrealistic solution to disarmament where
children shame political leaders into it.

012.   Bishop, Claire Huchet.   TWENTY AND TEN. Illustrated by
William Pene du Bois. New York: Viking Press, 1952; Penguin
Press, 1978, 76 pp. (ages 7-adult).

        Combining the Jewish flight from the Nazis during World
War II with a play-acting out of Jesus' flight from Egypt,
Claire Huchet Bishop has written an excellent story for
children about twenty French children (all in fifth grade,
except Louis, who is only four) who have been brought into the
school by Sister Gabriel to protect them from the war. One
day a young man appears with ten Jewish children and a
request: will Sister Gabriel and the ten non-Jewish children
staying with her hide and care for the ten Jewish children.
The Jewish children are hidden in the caves behind the school.
The Nazis come and take Sister Gabriel away and then attempt
to get the non-Jewish children to tell them where the Jewish
children are hidden.
        The subsequent story, based on a true story, provides a
good example of what children can do when placed in a
demanding position.

013.   Blanchard, Peter. JED: THE STORY OF A YANKEE SOLDIER AND
A SOUTHERN BOY. Illustrated by the author. New York: Coward,
1960 (ages 12-16).

        Jed, sixteen, has grown tired of the fighting and the
raiding of farms and plantations for food and supplies,
especially when the targets are women and children. His
disallusionment leads him to prevent a small party of his
fellow soldiers lead by Davy, a less conscientious soldier,
from raiding the farm of a small boy and his mother.
        Jed is a good representation of those who manage to
retain some of their decency in the midst of war, though the
story would be better if his character were more fully
developed.

014.   Blume, Judy.   TIGER EYES. New York: Laurel-Leaf Books,
1982, 222 pp. (ages 12-16).

        In addition to the standard attempts at sociology or
bibliotherapy common to the books of Judy Blume (in this case,
how to deal with the violent death of a loved one), TIGER EYES
offers a subtle statement on the frightening reality of the
arms race and the delicate balance between world peace and
world obliteration.
        After her father is killed while being robbed, Tiger Eyes
moves with her mother and brother to stay with her aunt and
uncle, until her mother can get herself back together. Tiger
Eyes' Uncle Walter is a very important scientist at Los
Alamos, involved with the continuing development of nuclear
weapons.
        As the story unfolds, the community of scientists and
their families, which at first seems to be held tightly under

control, each of its members filled with an unusually strong
sense of civic responsibility, begins to show cracks (children
who are alcoholics, and so on), until Uncle Walter
(representing the men in control of nuclear weapons) loses
control, blowing up in an angry fit at Tiger Eyes.

By the end of the story, when Tiger Eyes moves back to
Atlantic City with her mother and brother, and tells her Aunt
Betsy not to worry because "We're going to be all right," the
reader is aware of the dual meanings of that statement (i.e.,
Tiger Eye's family is going to be all right, and the universal
"we" is going to be all right in the context of possible
nuclear war), and the irony is apparent.

The characters, as is usual in Judy Blume's books, are
somewhat two-dimensional, meant to serve her sociological
purposes more than to be "real people," and the plot is very
predictable, but the subtlety of the nuclear war theme is more
sophisticated than she usually produces.

015.   Bonsall, Crosby. MINE'S THE BEST. New York: Harper &
Row, 1973, 32 pp. (ages 3-6).

A standard "I Can Read Book," meant for young children,
this is a short story about two boys who fight over who has
the better balloon, eventually destroying each other's
balloon. At the same time, though the boys don't notice it,
there is a special sale on balloons identical to their
balloons. Finally, a girl walks by with a balloon identical
to theirs, and they align with one another, saying "Ours was
the best."

The illustrations (apparently also by Crosby Bonsall) are
simple line drawings with flesh colors to indicate skin color.
They go well with the simplicity of the language and the
straight forward theme presentation.

016.   Bowers, Terrell L. SINCLAIR'S DOUBLE WAR. New York:
Avalon Books, 1984, 182 pp. (ages 9-12).

After the Civil War, Wayne Sinclair returned to Sunset,
New Mexico, hoping to forget the time he had spent in
Andersonville Prison. But the hate and prejudice that was
part of the war still existed.

Though this is little more than a standard, action-packed
western; it does offer some insights into the aftermath of the
Civil War.

017.   Boufet de Monvel, M. JOAN OF ARC. New York: The Century
Company, 1912, 47 pp. (ages 5-8).

This is a well illustrated (in fine line and color),
highly complimentary, brief history of Joan of Arc. The story
is told simply and in a straight forward manner. The
illustrations are highly detailed and realistic.

018.   Brewton, Sara and John E. Brewton and John Brewton
Blackburn. OF QUARKS, QUASARS, AND OTHER QUIRKS: QUIZZICAL
POEMS FOR THE SUPERSONIC AGE. Illustrated by Quentin Blake.
New York: Thomas Y. Crowell, 1977, 108 pp. (all ages).

This is a collection of "fun" poems for children and adults that have some connection with science and modern life, and includes some poems about nuclear war and its effects-- most notably Kenneth Burke's "If All the Thermo-Nuclear Warheads."

The illustrations and, indeed, the entire book, have a Shel Silverstein quality of irreverence.

019. Briggs, Raymond. THE TIN-POT FOREIGN GENERAL AND THE OLD IRON WOMAN. Boston: Little Brown, 1984, 48 pp. (all ages).

Master picture book creator Raymond Briggs has brought his talents to an anti-war picture book, satirizing the battle between England and Venezuela over the Faulkland Islands.

The book is filled with a collage of illustration styles, from the bold cartoon characterizations of Mother England and the Foreign General (slap-stick presentations filled with sex and violence) to the sombering black-and-white pencil drawings of wounded and dead people.

This wildly innovative and visually overwhelming "picture book" seems the product of a brilliant artist out of control. The anti-war messages are obvious, but the audience is not. Is this brutal, orgastic experience for children? If Dr. Seuss's BUTTER BATTLE BOOK raises a few eyebrows and questions about audience, this book will blast those same eyebrows right off the forehead.

Perhaps it's time to start speaking of picture books for adults and place this, along with Maruki's HIROSHIMA NO PIKA, in this "new" genre.

020. Briggs, Raymond. WHEN THE WIND BLOWS. New York: Schocken Books, 1982, 40 pp. (all ages).

This picture book about nuclear war employs Raymond Briggs cartoon style illustrations to follow the somewhat inept James and Hilda Boggs, who are meant to represent a typical older couple completely naive about nuclear war. Yet, suddenly, the apocalypse is upon them, and they bumble about, trying to recite some Bible passages before their imminent deaths.

The tone is bitterly ironic, resulting in a shocking "picture book," filled with tough, effective, sardonic humor. The message is obvious. The audience is not. Is this book for children? At first, Raymond Briggs thought not (too depressing). Instead, it appeared on an adult list, and received good reviews. However, children's book stores began selling it--and it was successful.

Obviously, its success in a children's book market raises questions about what is appropriate reading material for children.

021. Browning, Robert. "How They Brought the Good New from Ghent to Aix." 1845; rpt. p. 149, THE GOLDEN TREASURY OF POETRY. ed., Louis Untermeyer. Illustrated by Joan Walsh Anglund. New York: Golden Press, 1959, 324 pp. (all ages).

Three men race to bring the good news from Ghent to Aix, some ninety miles, during the war between some Dutch states,

under William of Orange, and Philip II of Spain. Only one of
them, Roland, arrives. Just what this important new is is
left untold.

022. Browning, Robert. "Incident of the French Camp,"; rpt.,
p. 148, THE GOLDEN TREASURY OF POETRY. ed., Louis Untermeyer.
Illustrated by Joan Walsh Anglund. New York: Golden Press,
1959, 324 pp. (all ages).

   Highly respected nineteenth century poet, Robert Browning
wrote this imaginary episode about a messenger's meeting with
Napoleon during Napoleon's attack on Ratisbon.
   It presents a clear, bold picture of Napoleon, and
concludes with the dramatic death of the messenger.

023. Bruckner, Karl. THE DAY OF THE BOMB. Translated by
Frances Lobb. New York: D. Van Nostrand, 1962, 191 pp. (ages
12-adult).

   Basing his story on Sadako Sasaki, the real life
twelve-year-old girl who died of leukemia as a result of the
bombing of Hiroshima and who now has a statue dedicated to her
in Peace Park, Japan, Karl Bruckner gives a fictionalized
account of the bombing of Hiroshima and the subsequent trials
Sadako's family went through, including the famous story of
the thousand paper cranes, an ancient symbol of hope and peace
in Japan and a current symbol of anti-nuclear activity.
   The book received the Austrian National Prize for
Juvenile Literature in 1961 and the city of Vienna Juvenile
Book Prize. It is a straight forward account of the human
side of an event which truly changed the course of history.
The "facts" of the bombing are detailed and accurate, but the
center of the story is the presentation of the human suffering
and hope that goes beyond the statistics. After reading the
story of the devastation of Hiroshima and of Sadako's struggle
for life, the reader can more fully appreciate the warning
offered on the final page:

         In the Peach Park in Hiroshima there is a monu-
         ment. Above a symbol representing the atom-bomb
         stands a bronze statue of Sadako Sasaki. Her
         hands, outstretched towards heaven, are holding
         a golden stork.
         The erection of this monument, many feet high,
         was made possible by subscriptions from Japanese
         schoolboys and girls from all over the country.
         By means of this warning symbol they hoped to
         appeal to fathers and mothers all over the world.
         "Remember Sadako Sasaki! Think of your own child-
         ren. Don't say, 'It is wiser not to tell our
         children anything of what happened.' It is not
         wiser! For anyone who ignores the peril is likely
         to die of it. Remember, too, that a thousand
         hydrogen bombs are lying in readiness! The de-
         structive force of one such bomb is a thousand
         times greater that (sic) that of the uranium bomb
         which destroyed Hiroshima in a matter of seconds."

024. Buck, Pearl S. MATTHEW, MARK, LUKE, AND JOHN.
Illustrated by Mamoru Funai. New York: John Day, 1967, 80 pp.
(ages 8-12).

     This is an overly simplistic story about four
illegitimate Korean-born boys of American fathers who have
been abandoned and forced to fend for themselves by stealing,
until a nice American meets them and finds them American
families. The illustrations are sketchy line drawings with
slight shading. They add very little, if anything, to the
story. Both the illustrations and the story romanticize the
horrors of the aftermath of the Korean War.

025. Bunting, Eve. TERRIBLE THINGS. Illustrated by Stephen
Gammell. New York: Harper & Row, 1980, 26 pp. (ages 5-8).

     Here is an excellent fable about selfishness. The forest
is peaceful, until the "Terrible Things" come and, one by one,
take away the creatures. Each time, the other species do not
try to help whichever species is being taken, but rather, they
make excuses for not helping, until only one rabbit remains.
He leaves for another forest, where he will try to explain the
"Terrible Things" in hope that someone will listen.
     The illustrations, in black-and-white, are excellent and
help give the story its scary overtones.
     Eve Bunting has written several books for children. ONE
MORE FLIGHT won the Golden Kite award of the Society of
Children's Book Writers in 1977, and this book lives up to her
reputation as an excellent children's writer.

026. Burke, Kenneth. "If All the Thermo-Nuclear Warheads," p.
23, OF QUARKS, QUASARS, AND OTHER QUIRKS: QUIZZICAL POEMS FOR
THE SUPERSONIC AGE. Edited by Sara Brewton and John Brewton
and John Brewton Blackburn. Illustrated by Quentin Blake. New
York: Thomas Y. Crowell, 1977. Brewton, Sara.

     This is an "if" poem on what would happen if the greatest
military man dropped a great nuclear warhead on a great land
mass.

027. Caldwell, John C. LET'S VISIT VIETNAM. New York: John
Day, 1966, 96 pp. (ages 8-12).

     John C. Caldwell, author of COMMUNISM IN OUR WORLD,
offers here a strongly anti-communist, domino theory of the
Vietnam war. He states:

               In 1954, our government made a pledge not only
          to help the people of Vietnam, but to protect the
          country from its enemies. If the United States
          were to break its promise, thousands and perhaps
          millions of innocent people would be murdered or
          sent to communist prisons. The United States has
          also promised to defend Thailand and the Phili-
          pines. If Vietnam were conquered by the commu-
          nists, we might soon have to fight to help these
          other nations who have been promised American
          protection. All of Asia would be threatened.

A great deal of interesting detail of the culture is included, as are several good black-and-white photographs. Nevertheless, I would hope anyone reading this book would also read some books offering another perspective (e.g., Betty Jean Lifton and Thomas C. Fox's CHILDREN OF VIETNAM or Milton Meltzer's AIN'T GONNA STUDY WAR NO MORE: THE STORY OF AMERICAN PEACE SEEKERS).

028. Carle, Eric. DO YOU WANT TO BE MY FRIEND? Illustrated by the author. New York: Thomas Y. Crowell, 1971, 30 pp. (ages 3-5).

At the beginning a mouse asks "Do you want to be my friend?" Then the book follows the mouse as it encounters several animals (no words). Finally, the mouse meets another mouse, who answers "Yes."

029. Carle, Eric. THE GROUCHY LADYBUG. Illustrated by the author. New York: Thomas Y. Crowell, 1977, 40 pp. (ages 3-5).

Grouchy Ladybug tries to pick a fight with various characters, finally ending up where she started, saying thanks to another ladybug for sharing a leaf. Carle's variation on page size reflect the passing of time, and his bright colors help get across a strong anti-fighting message.

030. Carr, Albert. MEN OF POWER: A BOOK OF DICTATORS. Illustrated by Marc Simont. New York: Viking Press, 1940, 272 pp. (ages 10-15).

Written during the early years of World War II, this book discusses nine powerful dictators: Richelieu, Cromwell, Frederick, Napoleon, Bolivar, Bismarck, Mussolini, Stalin, and Hitler. There is a condescending tone to it, and it is highly pro-democracy--not unexpected considering the date it was published.
A postscript explains the value of a democracy, ending with the first sentence of The Declaration of Independence.

031. Carr, Albert. A MATTER OF LIFE AND DEATH: HOW WARS GET STARTED--OR ARE PREVENTED. New York: Viking Press, 1966, 256 pp. (ages 12-adult).

In an "Open Letter to Kathy and John Jay Carr, and Jane Kingsbury," Albert Carr points out the seriousness of war and the hope it will not occur again. The book, he says, is not meant to entertain but to offer a "shock of awareness." It is meant to put forth cold, hard facts and raise questions--which it does.
It gives a history of American wars, along with how they might have been avoided, and it discusses patriotism and several alternatives to war. Included are a brief, selected reading list, generally on twentieth century conflicts, a good section of references and notes for each chapter, and an index.

032.   Catton, Bruce, et al. THE GOLDEN BOOK OF THE CIVIL WAR.
Adapted for young readers by Charles Flato from THE AMERICAN
HERITAGE PICTURE HISTORY OF THE CIVIL WAR. New York: Golden
Press, 1960, 216 pp. (ages 12-17).

     This large format book, packed full with outstanding
color and black-and-white illustrations, photographs, maps,
and so on, presents an easily understood overview of the Civil
War.   An excellent, detailed chronology of the Civil War is
included, as well as an index.
     Unfortunately, Bruce Catton's "Introduction" has a
condescending tone, as does much of his narrative, that would
possibly turn off a junior high school reader, who I assume
the book is aimed at.   Nevertheless, it is a worthwhile
introduction to the facts of the war.

033.   Chaikin, Miriam. AVIVA'S PIANO. Illustrated by Yossi
Abolafia. New York: Houghton Mifflin, 1986, 43 pp. (ages 5-8).

     This picture book offers a Jewish view of life in
contemporary war torn Israel.   Aviva, who is in third grade,
got a piano, but it would not fit into her house.
Fortunately, a bomb blew a hole in the side of her house, and
she was then able to move the piano inside.   This strange good
result of bombing, however, may offer a false view of war to a
child.   Also, the matter-of-fact acceptance of war--though,
perhaps, honest--suggests it as inevitable (as if one, at
least a Jew, should accept the fate of eternal suffering).
     Some of the Jewish terms would be difficult for
non-Jewish readers, though many of them are defined, and the
others may lead readers to learn some new words and gain a bit
more understanding of Jewish culture.
     Yossi Abolafia is a well known animator/illustrator, but
his illustrations here are of a "cartoonist" nature,
suggesting a "Leave It to Beaver" life not consistent with the
reality.

034.   "THE CHARGE OF THE LIGHT BRIGADE" AND OTHER STORY POEMS.
No editor indicated. New York: Scholastic Book Services, 1969.
(ages 8-adult).

     This is an excellent collection of story poems, some of
them dealing with war, i.e., "Barbara Frietche" by John
Greenleaf Whittier.

035.   Clapp, Patricia. I'M DEBORAH SAMPSON: A SOLDIER IN THE
REVOLUTIONARY WAR. New York: Lothrop, Lee & Shepard, 1977, 176
pp. (ages 10-adult).

     Based on a real person, this is the story of a woman who
disguised herself as a man and fought in the revolutionary
war.
     When her poor mother can no longer support her, Deborah
goes to work on a farm, where she gains the strength and
determination she will later need for her ordeals ahead.
After her two adopted brothers leave home to fight in the
revolution, and one gets killed, she disguises herself as a
man and spends three years hiding her identity and living in a

masculine world, more worried about the discovery of her
identity then death itself.
    Deborah's character is well developed, and the plot,
though containing no real surprises, is suspenseful. Teenage
girls should be especially attracted to the book.

036. Clapp, Patricia. THE TAMARACK TREE: A NOVEL OF THE SIEGE
OF VICKSBURG. New York: Lothrop, Lee & Shepard, 1986,
211 pp. (12-adult).

    Rosemary Leigh, the main character and teller of the
story, came to Vicksburg, Mississippi, from England in 1859.
Four years later, at the age of eighteen, while she and her
friends are under attack in the forty-seven-day siege of
Vicksbury, she writes about her experiences growing-up in the
South. Her perspective is unique, since she comes from
England, and her loyalities are mixed, since she loves the
social world of the South but hates the idea of slavery (not
an uncommon feeling today about the Old South).
    This is an excellent historical novel (romance) that
should be well received by young women.

037. Clark, Leonard, ed. DRUMS AND TRUMPETS. Illustrated by
Heather Copley. Philadelphia: Dufour Editions, 1962, 95 pp.
(all ages).

    This is an eclectic collection of poetry for children
that includes several poems on war, many of them dealing with
the pageantry of it, but some, such as Thomas Hardy's "Men Who
March Away," suggesting a darker side to it.
    The illustrations, line drawings in dark gray, are
scattered across each page.

038. Clayton, Ed. MARTIN LUTHER KING: THE PEACEFUL WARRIOR.
Illustrated by David Hodges. Enlarged Edition. Englewood
Cliffs, N.J.: Prentice-Hall, 1964, 87 pp. (ages 8-14).

    This excellent, straightforward introduction to the
important events in Martin Luther King, Jr.'s, life contains
passages, such as the following, stressing his belief in
passive resistance:

        "If you have weapons," Dr. King said to them
        quietly, "take them home. If you do not have
        them, please do not seek to get them. We cannot
        solve this problem through violence . . . Remember
        the words of Jesus: 'He who lives by the sword shall
        perish by the sword.' . . . We must meet our white
        brothers' hate with love."

    It is a book about more than Martin Luther King, Jr.--as
any good book about him should be--it is a book about peace.

039. Clemens, Samuel Langhorne. (See Mark Twain).

040. Clifton, Lucille. AMIFIKA. New York: Dutton, 1977, 28
pp. (ages 5-8).

     Amifika is a black child whose father has been away, in
the army, for a long time, but now Amifika's father is coming
home. Amifika overhears his mother and cousin discussing all
of the things they are going to throw away and fears they will
also throw him away, because he cannot remember his father.
He hides in the yard, falls asleep, and wakens to a warm
embrace from his father.
     Lucille Clifton's writing is excellent, capturing the
dialect, i.e., "Oh, Katy, Katy, got a letter from Albert and
he be home tomorrow for good!" And the soft black-and-white
illustrations by Thomas DiGrazia express real characters in a
real house, extending the text tremendously.
     It is a well done picture book, expressing one of the
often over looked effects of war--the separation of soldiers
from their families.

041. Coerr, Elanor. SADAKO AND THE THOUSAND PAPER CRANES.
Illustrated by Ronald Himler. New York: Putnam, 1977, 64 pp.
(ages 8-12).

     In 1955, Sadako, a thirteen-year-old Japanese girl, died
of "the atom bomb disease"--radiation-induced leukemia. She
was but one of many children to suffer from the after-effects
of the atomic bomb dropped on Hiroshima, August 6, 1945, but
she was the one who became a symbol for peace, and several
books have been written about her.
     This book follows her from just before she got leukemia,
when she was still healthy and a fast runner, through her
sickness, when she tried to fold a thousand paper cranes in
order to fulfill a Japanese myth that says that cranes live
for a thousand years, and that the person who folds a thousand
paper cranes will have her wish granted, which in Sadako's
case was to recover from her sickness. Sadako only managed to
fold 644 cranes before she died. Her classmates folded the
remaining 356, so she could be buried with 1,000.
     Subsequently, money was collected to build a monument to
Sadako in Hiroshima's Peace Park with the inscription: "This
is our cry, This is our prayer, Peace in the world."
     The statue and the folding of paper cranes have become a
world wide symbol for anti-nuclear activities.
     The writing in this version matches the simplicity of the
emotions involved, creating a moving experience. The
black-and-white illustrations are not impressive.

042. Cohen, Barbara. THE SECRET GROVE. Illustrated by Michael
J. Deraney. New York: Union of American Hebrew Congragations,
1985, 28 pp. (ages 8-10).

     Beni, a Jewish boy, tells a story about secretly meeting
Ahmed, an Arab boy (the enemy), when they are in fifth grade
and becoming friends with him. The words and style of writing
are a bit difficult for children under twelve, though the
story and illustrations seem to be aimed at younger children.
     Other than that, however, it is an excellent story that
questions the prejudice separating the Middle East today.

043. Cole, William, ed. I'M MAD AT YOU. Illustrated by George
MacClain. New York: Collins & World, 1978, 67 pp. (ages 6-9).

        This is a good collection of poems on hate and conflict
by such highly respected poets as Jack Prelutsky, Shel
Silverstein and John Ciardi.

044. Collier, James Lincoln and Christopher Collier. THE
BLOODY COUNTRY. New York: Four Winds Press, 1976, 183 pp.
(ages 12-adult).

        The authors, using their expertise in early American
history, recreate the mid-eighteenth century property conflict
between Connecticut and Pennsylvania, including the massacre
of Connecticut settlers by the British and their Indian and
Tory allies, resulting in the senseless murder of hundreds of
people.
        This is one of several excellent books by these brothers
on early American history, including the Newbery Honor book,
MY BROTHER SAM IS DEAD.

045. Collier, James Lincoln and Christopher Collier. MY
BROTHER SAM IS DEAD. New York: Four Winds Press, 1974, 216 pp.
(ages 12-adult).

        This Newbery Honor book about the Revolutionary War deals
with the tragedy that strikes the Meeker family when one son
(Sam) joins the rebel forces while the rest of the family
tries to stay neutral in a Tory town.
        Sam's brother Tom narrates the story. Both Sam and his
father are killed, examples of the ugliness and hardship and
waste of war, though the war itself is not presented as either
right or wrong, nor are sides taken. The book ends:

                It will be, I am sure, a great history. Free of
                British domination, the nation has prospered and I
                along with it. Perhaps on some other anniversary
                of the United States somebody will read this and
                see what the cost has been. Father said, "In war
                the dead pay the debts of the living," and they
                have paid as well. But somehow, even fifty years
                later, I keep thinking that there might have been
                another way, besides war, to achieve the same end.

        The brothers' expertise in Early American history is
evident in the details, and they include a discussion at the
end of the book, pointing out the authenticity of their
material.

046. Collier, James Lincoln and Christopher Collier. WAR
COMES TO WILLY FREEMAN. New York: Delacorte Press, 1983, 178
pp. (ages 12-adult).

        One of several books by these two brothers dealing with
the revolutionary war, this follows a free thirteen-year-old
black girl in Connecticut, who is caught up in the horrors of
the Revolutionary War and the dangers of being returned to
slavery when her patriot father is killed by the British and

her mother disappears.
    Christopher Collier's expertise is evident in the
authenticity of the details. The authors have included a
brief discussion at the end of the book discussing their
attempts to be accurate and to capture the flavor of the
times, including a brief defense of the use of the word
"nigger."
    Most of the characters are based on real people and are
fully drawn.

047. Collier, James Lincoln and Christopher Collier. THE
WINTER HERO. New York: Four Winds Press, 1978, 152 pp. (ages
12-adult).

    This, as the authors briefly explain at the end of the
book, is an attempt to reconstruct Shay's Rebellion, began by
farmers in western Massachusetts to protest the unfair
taxation levied on them by the Boston government, 1786-87.
Except for Justin Conkey, the young boy who tells the story,
the major characters are based on real people. The historical
detail is excellent.
    In addition, the book raises questions about fighting and
the use of violence to achieve positive ends, as the final
paragraph indicates:

> . . . If there hadn't been a rebellion, maybe
> nobody much in western Massachusetts would have
> got fired up enough to go out and vote. This
> was a question I never could decide. Would we
> ever have got our grievances redressed if we had-
> n't shown the government that we were willing to
> fight?

048. Cook, Paul. DUENDE MEADOW. New York: Bantam, 1985, 240
pp. (ages 12-18).

    The American military threatens nuclear holocaust, and
the hope for survival lies at the hands of peaceful and
friendly, non-communist Russian refugees who have settled in
Kansas.
    It is an interesting concept. However, the books is hard
to take seriously, as the situation is so over-simplified--the
national leaders too stupid, the military too evil.

049. Coolidge, Olivia. THE APPRENTICESHIP OF ABRAHAM LINCOLN.
New York: Scribner, 1972, 242 pp. (ages 14-adult).

    Though mainly known for her work on mythology, Olivia
Coolidge has also achieved recognition for several
biographies, some dealing with men and/or events connected
with war. Some are both, i.e., MARATHON LOOKS AT THE SEA is
about Metiochos and is set against the Battle of Marathon.
    THE APPRENTICESHIP OF ABRAHAM LINCOLN and its companion
book, THE STATESMANSHIP OF ABRAHAM LINCOLN, New York:
Scribner, 1977, 237 pp. (ages 14-adult), offer a highly
researched view of both Lincoln and the times, and both are
recommended for older youth (a slightly younger audience
should turn to Russell Freedman's LINCOLN: A PHOTOBIOGRAPHY).

Some of Olivia Coolidge's other books dealing with war follow.

050. Coolidge, Olivia. CROMWELL'S HEAD. Illustrated by Edward A. Wilson. Boston: Houghton Mifflin, 1955, 262 pp. (ages 14-adult).

This story about James Gilroy, seventeen, apprenticed to Dr. Browne, a Tory, blends an intricate plot, a great deal of authentic detail, and a hard look at the realities, motives and opinions behind the American Revolution to offer teenagers (it's aimed at an older audience than Ester Forbes' JOHNNY TREMAIN) a colorful blend of history and romance.

051. Coolidge, Olivia. GANDHI. Boston: Houghton Mifflin, 1972, 278 pp. (ages 14-adult).

This is an excellent, fully realized picture of a great man who successfully lead a nation to freedom through passive resistance.

052. Coolidge, Olivia. MAKERS OF THE RED REVOLUTION. Boston: Houghton Mifflin, 1963, 240 pp. (ages 14-adult).

Factually correct biographies of the founders of communism, including Marx, Lenin, Trotsky, Stalin, Tito, Khruschev, and Mao, are offered in a straight forward manner ideal for introducing teenagers to the subject.

053. Coolidge, Olivia. MEN OF ATHENS. Illustrated by Milton Johnson. Boston: Houghton Mifflin, 1962, 244 pp. (ages 14-18).

Though not centered on war and peace, the book contains many short stories about important Athenians who lived during the conflict with Persia and the war with and defeat by the Peloponnesians.

054. Coolidge, Olivia. TOM PAINE, REVOLUTIONARY. New York: Charles Scribners Sons, 1969, 206 pp. (ages 10-16).

This is a completely researched, factual study of Thomas Paine, and offers a clear focus on both him and his times. A "Suggestions for Further Reading" and an "Index" are included.

055. Coolidge, Olivia. THE TROJAN WAR. Illustrated by Edouard Sandoz. Boston: Houghton Mifflin, 1952, 244 pp. (ages 12-adult).

This is an excellent retelling of the famous war drawn from THE ILIAD and THE ODYSSEY, and other ancient Greek works. It begins with the meeting of Paris and Helen, and offers a sequential story of the successive events.

056. Coolidge, Olivia. WINSTON CHURCHILL AND THE STORY OF TWO
WORLD WARS. Boston: Houghton Mifflin, 1960, 278 pp. (ages
14-up).

     As usual, Coolidge presents a well rounded, complex
individual---demanding reading.

057. Cormier, Robert. AFTER THE FIRST DEATH. New York: Avon,
1980, 223 pp. (ages 14-adult).

     A gripping narrative, as is normal for a Cormier book,
AFTER THE FIRST DEATH explores patriotism and courage,
betrayal and loyalty, power and its abuse--all within the
world of terrorism.
     A group of refugee "freedom fighters" take over a bus
load of children and make demands for the release of the
children: 1) a cash ransom; 2) the release of some political
prisoners, and 3) the tearing down of a top-secret United
States Army installation.
     Then, when General Marchand, head of the army operation,
chooses his fifteen-year-old son to act as go between, three
young adults with differing perspectives are juxtaposed--Kate
Forrester, the bus driver; Miro Shantas, a sixteen-year-old
terrorist, and Ben Marchand, the general's son.
     As is characteristic in Cormier, the novel shifts through
various narrators (at times becoming confusing), and within
this technique slowly reveals the characters' personalities,
creating real people--all of them somewhat naive about their
motives, each of the three main characters trying to live up
to some ideal adults have thrust on them, resulting in a story
that pushes forward, uncompromisingly, to a blunt finality
where children (young adults) torture and kill one another in
a terrifying confrontation with the nightmare reality of
terriorism. It is a harshly ironic portrayal of the morally
complex and dark reality of the contemporary world, and
because of this, it is a controversial book for young people.

058. Cormier, Robert. I AM THE CHEESE. New York: Pantheon,
1977, 234 pp. (ages 14-adult).

     The story moves forward quietly. Adam Farmer, a
fourteen-year-old boy rides his bike to Vermont to visit his
father in the hospital and has various experiences along the
way. Some of the experiences are a bit frightening but not
overly so. Doesn't sound like a Cormier book. That's because
this is only the innocent (unknowing) surface. Underneath it
seethes the horrifying psychological journey of the same boy,
whose real name is Paul Delmonte, back into his past, as a
psychiatrist attempts to bring out stubbornly hidden memories.
The two stories proceed together in a typical Cormier style of
juxtaposition, revealing bits and pieces, building to a
powerful and terrifying conclusion.
     Cormier is a skilled craftsman and brutally
uncompromising in his world view--which can easily be said to
be a dark one. This is a complex novel, both in construction
and theme. For adolescents who are able to handle such
complexities, it will be a rewarding experience. It is not
for those who are looking for a happy ending.

059. Cowan, Lore. CHILDREN OF THE RESISTANCE. New York:
Hawthorn, 1969,   pp. (ages 12-adult).

Lore Cowan thoroughly researched incidents of resistance
by young people during the Nazi regime and has written a
collection of eight fictionalized stories (based strongly on
real incidents) to show that "not all the 'Young People' in
Europe climbed on Hitler's Bandwagon."
    Her statement in the "Preface" explains the value of the
book:

> My answer to that [the value of the book] is that
> the youth of today want to know, and need to be
> constantly reminded that freedom is precious, and
> that it is something that must, if necessary, be
> fought for, and that, in that fight for freedom
> throughout World War II, the children of the
> Resistance played a noble and significant part.
>   They will always be an example to the young
> people of today.

060. Cowley, Joy. THE DUCK IN THE GUN. Illustrated by Edward
Sorel. New York: Doubleday, 1969, 40 pp. (ages 5-adult).

This is an excellent, humorous book about a general who
marched his men around a town and decided it was time to
fight. However, the gunner informed the general the gun could
not be fired because there was a duck in it sitting on some
eggs (typical British humor). Unable to get the duck to come
out and unwilling to fire the gun while the duck was inside,
the general went to speak to the Prime Minister, who was the
enemy, about the gun, and suggested the two sides share the
one gun of the Prime Minister, since it would be unfair if
only one side had a gun, and of course, it would not be right
to remove the duck from the gun the general owned when it was
sitting on some eggs. However, the Prime Minister's gun would
be far too hard to move back and forth. Thus, a decision was
made to delay the war for three weeks, until the duck had had
its eggs.
    Then the general encountered yet another problem. He was
running out of money to pay his men for doing nothing. He
spoke with the Prime Minister about it, and a decision was
made to have the men paint the Prime Minister's town, which
was badly in need of it.
    In the meantime, the general fell in love with the Prime
Minister's daughter.
    By the time the three weeks had passed and the duck had
given birth to its ducklings no one was any longer in the mood
for a war, and it was put off for good. The general then
married the Prime Minister's daughter.
    The book is filled with humor, both in the text and in
the illustrations, some of which young children will
appreciate, some aimed at an older, adult audience, and almost
without being aware of it the readers gains a feeling for the
stupidity and waste of war and the positive ideas of talking
out one's problems.

061. Crane, Maureen. A BOAT TO NOWHERE. Illustrated by Dick
Teicher. Philadelphia: Westminster Press, 1980, 189 pp. (ages
10-adult).

    When the new communist government comes to their village
to take away Thay Van Chi and impose communist rule, Thay Van
Chi and three young children (Loe, Mai, and Kiem) flee by
boat.
    They experience many hardships (including Thay Van Chi's
death), until, eventually, the Camelot, a freighter, picks
them up.
    This is a realistic story about the boat people, lost and
without a country. Further, it offers an introduction to the
wisdom of the old Vietnamese.

062. Crane, Stephen. THE COMPLETE POEMS OF STEPHEN CRANE.
Edited by Joseph Katz. Ithaca, New York: Cornell University,
1972, 154 pp. (ages 10-adult).

    These poems, which broke new ground as a "free verse" or
"prose poetry," and serve as central works in American
Naturalism, express Crane's dark vision of the human race and
of war. Though THE RED BADGE OF COURAGE is what secondary
school students are usually exposed to, Crane claims to have
liked his poetry better (DeMOREST'S FAMILY MAGAZINE, XXXII,
May, 1896, pp. 399-400).
    This collection includes an excellent introduction by
Joseph Katz and an index of first lines. It is must reading,
especially "Do Not Weep, Maiden, for War is Kind."

063. Crane, Stephen. THE RED BADGE OF COURAGE AND SELECTED
STORIES. Edited and with an introduction and notes by R. W.
Stallman. New York: New American Library, 1980, 222 pp.
(ages 10-adult).

    THE RED BADGE OF COURAGE, an American "classic," first
published in 1895, is probably Stephen Crane's most celebrated
work and is often included in secondary school curriculums.
Its irony and paradoxes (key elements in Crane's style) allow
for multiple interpretations; however, there can be no doubt
but that it expresses a coldly realistic (naturalistic) view
of war and bravery.
    The story follows Henry Fleming (the youth), who leaves
home to join in the glorious conflict, finds war anything but
glorious, and in a moment of supreme irony "earns" his red
badge of courage while fleeing from battle.
    It is must reading!
    This particular edition also includes Crane's more famous
short stories: "The Upturned Face," "The Open Boat," "The
Blue Hotel," and "The Bride Comes To Yellow Sky"--all
excellent examples of naturalism, especially "The Open Boat."
    There is a brief "Foreward" by R. W. Stillman, "Notes" on
the text, and a "Selected Bibliography" of Crane's writings
and of biography and criticism on Crane.

064. Cummings, Betty Sue. HEW AGAINST THE GRAIN. New York:
Atheneum, 1977, 174 pp. (ages 12-16).

    This is a complex historical-romance of the Civil War,
centering on Matilda Repass, who is twelve at the start, and
her family, who experience death, injury and rape.

065. Dank, Milton. THE DANGEROUS GAME. New York: J. B.
Lippincott, 1977, 155 pp. (ages 12-adult).

    Milton Dank served in France as a combat glider pilot
with the United States First Airborne Army in 1944-45 and as a
squadron translator and liaison officer with the French civil
authorities after the Liberation, and subsequently authored
THE FRENCH AGAINST THE FRENCH, a work of non-fiction about
this time period. His knowledge of the Nazi occupation is
evident in the realistic details of THE DANGEROUS GAME, which
leads the reader through the French Resistance Movement.
    The main character, Charles, a sixteen-year-old boy,
joins the resistance movement shortly after the Nazi invasion
of 1940, and he experiences a real world of spies, traitors,
and death. Seventeen by the end of the novel, he attempts to
tell his mother what he has been through:

            His mother gasped and turned her head away to
            hide the tears. Charles persisted in describing
            what had happened in the rue Lauriston. He wanted
            her to understand, to hear everything. "Oh yes,
            Maman, I killed them. Pascal was a traitor and
            a threat to all of us. The Nazi just get in the
            way."
                He continued his story in a matter-of-fact
            voice.

    Later, in an unemotional voice, he read off the list he
had just received of his comrades, captured and condemned to
death by a German military tribunal for "espionage and acts of
violence against Germany."

066. Dank, Milton. GAME'S END. New York: J. B. Lippincott,
1979, 158 pp. (ages 12-adult).

    This is a sequel to THE DANGEROUS GAME. Charles Marceau,
now a second lieutenant in the Free French Army, returns to
the French resistance movement in preparation for the allied
invasion.
    As with his other novels, this is a well written, fast
paced tale that presents some of the dilemmas of war.

067. Dank, Milton. KHAKI WINGS. New York: Delacorte Press,
1980, 180 pp. (ages 12-adult).

    Once again, Milton Dank presents an action packed novel
of pilots, this time pilots of World War I. In this story,
Edward Burton signs up for pilot training in the new Royal
Flying Corps. At first, he finds it a great adventure, but
soon he faces the frightening reality.
    Moral dilemmas are brought to life.

068.   Dank, Milton. RED FLIGHT TWO. New York: Delacorte Press,
1981, 185 pp. (ages 10-adult).

This sequel to KHAKI WINGS follows pilot Edward Burton,
who begins the story as a flight instructor in England. It is
the autumn of 1916. Burton, at age 18, has already served two
years as a pilot, won seven victories in the air, received
medals--and suffered a nervous breakdown caused by watching
Iain, his best friend, die.
     The story unfolds quickly. Burton returns to the battle
in France, where he finds himself, once again, in command of
his old squadron--deciding which men to send out to likely
death.
     It is a fast-paced adventure story, but it is more.
Burton's struggles with his "moral responsibilities" reveal
the hard to answer ethical dilemmas for leaders during times
of combat.

069.   Dareff, Hal. FROM VIETNAM TO CAMBODIA: A BACKGROUND BOOK
ABOUT THE STRUGGLE IN SOUTHEAST ASIA. New York: Parents'
Magazine Press, 1971, 196 pp. (ages 12-adult).

Written shortly before the official end of the Vietnam
War, this sequel to THE STORY OF VIETNAM offers an opinionated
political and social history of Vietnam and Cambodia from 1966
through 1970.

070.   Daugherty, James. ABRAHAM LINCOLN. New York: Viking
Press, 1943, 209 pp. (ages 10-14).

This version of Lincoln's biography by James Daugherty,
writer/illustrator of many children's books, has a gaudy feel.
The illustrations in two-color lithography are bold, filled
with action, and have a characature quality. The writing
contains the diction and rhythms of a frontier storyteller.
All this makes for a fast-paced romp through Lincoln's life.
     The book ends with the following verses in remembrance of
Lincoln from Walt Whitman's "When Lilacs Last in the Dooryard
Bloom'd":

              When lilacs last in the dooryard bloom'd,
              And the great star early droop'd in the western
                 sky in the night,
              I mourn'd, and yet shall mourn with ever-returning
                 spring.

              Ever-returning spring, trinity sure to me you
                 bring,
              Lilac blooming perennial and drooping star in the
                 west,
              And thought of him I love.

                  *   *   *   *   *   *   *   *

              In the dooryard fronting an old farm-house near
                 the white-wash'd palings.
              Stands the lilac-bush tall-growing with heart
              -shaped leaves of rich green,
              With many a pointed blossom rising delicate, with

```
         the perfume strong I love,
    With every leaf a miracle--and from this bush in
         the dooryard,
    With delicate-color'd blossoms and heart-shaped
         leaves of rich green,
    A sprig with its flower I break.
```

For a discussion of Whitman's poem turn to that entry.

071. D'Aulaire, Ingri and Edgar Parin D'Aulaire. ABRAHAM
LINCOLN. New York: Doubleday, 1939, 58 pp. (ages 7-10).

     In her Caldecott Medal acceptance speech, after pointing
out the tragedy of the world plunging rapidly into World War
II, Ingri Parin D'Aulaire states that, as she and her husband
got deeper and deeper into their research for this book, they:

          became more and more convinced that if only we
          could give to our young readers a bit of the
          feeling we had about Abraham Lincoln we had per-
          haps done our tiny share to make the world a
          happier place, when those who are now children
          have grown up to run the world.

     In this way, she brings together the continual human
condition of war and the desire to rise above it. And the
final page of ABRAHAM LINCOLN contains Lincoln's famous line:
"with malice towards none, with charity to all"--a thought
worth considering.
     The book, written and illustrated by two Norwegians known
for their knowledge and love of Norway, gains significance
because, as Edgar Parin D'Aulaire states in his Caldecott
acceptance speech:

          We are here in this country not because we
          were born here but because the whole world was
          ours to choose from and we chose America as our
          home and our country. . . . where we could fulfill
          our full measures as human beings and help in
          building up the world.

     The book has been rightfully praised for the warm depth
of its illustrations (which have the soft, fuzzy quality
common to illustrations of the time) and for the accuracy of
the text. It is a good book for younger children.

072. D'Aulaire, Ingri and Edgar Parin D'Aulaire. GEORGE
WASHINGTON. New York: Doubleday, 1936, 56 pp. (ages 3-6).

     Done in D'Aulaire's standard style, the lithograph
illustrations (often taking up an entire page) have a simple
childishness about them (a vague similarity to American Naive
paintings). The sentences are short; the diction is easy to
follow. Perhaps, it simplicity is overdone (and becomes a
talking-down to children), but young children should find the
book a good introduction to George Washington.

073. Davies, Andrew. CONRAD'S WAR. Great Britain, 1978; New York: Crown, 1980, 120 pp. (ages 8-12).

Conrad feels neglected. He loves war and guns and violence and wishes his parents would let him watch more of it on television. He decides to build a tank out of bicycle wheels, cardboard, and wood.
Then he falls into a dream and enters World War II, where he meets his dad. For a while, he enjoys it, but then the dream turns, and he becomes the enemy.
It's a strange book, filled with both pathos and humor, and bizarre twists, some of which might be hard for younger readers to follow.

074. Davis, Burke. GEORGE WASHINGTON AND THE AMERICAN REVOLUTION. New York: Random House, 1975, 497 pp. (ages 14-adult).

In a generally fast-paced narrative, Burke Davis reveals the human side of Washington and the American Revolution-- though the reader may still feel a sense of not really "knowing" Washington. The maps are easy to read and help to reveal the action.

075. Davis, Daniel S. BEHIND BARBED WIRE; THE IMPRISONMENT OF JAPANESE AMERICANS DURING WORLD WAR II. New York: Dutton, 1982, 166 pp. (ages 10-15).

Beginning with the bombing of Pearl Harbor, Daniel S. Davis, who has written several books on prejudice, demonstrates how the subsequent hysteria that swept the United States had a solid foundation in the history of the country. The book is a well research revealing of what children are seldom introduced to--a sad chapter in United States history.

076. Degens, T. THE GAME ON THATCHER ISLAND. New York: Viking Press, 1977, 148 pp. (ages 10-adult).

Harry joins the Morrison boys for a secret "war game" on Thatcher Island. He is flattered to be asked (a chance to be one of the big boys). However, things don't go as he planned. His sister Sarah finds out, and John, The Fresh Air Fund boy, arrives.
Harry takes them along (he has no choice), "borrows" his father's whaler, ends up with Sarah and John anchored near Thatcher Island, and is shocked to find out that he, Sarah, and John are the "enemy."
The cruelty of the war games, which Harry, in his pride and anger, joins, brings out the dark side of human nature. Though it cannot be considered as outstanding a book as William Golding's LORD OF THE FLIES, the similarities are there.

077. Degens, T. TRANSPORT 7-41-R. New York: Viking Press, 1974, 171 pp. (ages 12-adult).

This highly praised novel, winner of the first Inter-

national Reading Association Children's Book Award and the
Horn Book Award, and listed as an American Library Association
Notable Book, follows the travels of a thirteen-year-old from
the Russian sector of defeated Germany to Cologne on a transport carrying returning refugees in 1946.

As the journey unfolds, the lives of the various characters are also unfolded, and the destruction of war is well
communicated. This is a book that should be read.

078. Degens, T. THE VISIT. New York: Viking Press, 1982.
(ages 12-adult).

This novel, dealing with the implications of war, takes
place at a family gathering in Berlin years after World War
II. Kate's father happens upon an old notebook, a diary, kept
by his now dead sister Kate and gives it to his daughter Kate.
Kate relives some of the events of the now dead aunt, who was
once forced to be a member of the Hitler Youth, and gains a
new view of her living Aunt Sylvia, who was an 'overly energetic' member of the group and, it is implied, caused Aunt
Kate's death.

Until she read the diary, Kate had always liked her Aunt
Sylvia, but now the diary has shown Kate an evil, selfish side
to Aunt Sylvia. The book ends:

> I close the notebook and lock it in my desk.
> I have decided what to do. I owe it to Kate and
> myself and maybe even to Aunt Sylvia. She will
> be in her room after the broken-up seance.
> "I know what happened to your sister Kate of
> Camp Dechevow," I will say to Aunt Sylvia. "I
> have read the other Kate's diary." The words
> will scratch my throat, but I no longer care
> about her answer.

079. Dehkes, Evelyn S. THE YOUNG VIKING WARRIOR: A STORY OF
THE NINTH CENTURY. Illustrated by John Moment. New York:
Bobbs-Merrill, 1953, 211 pp. (ages 10-15).

This is what is generally referred to as a boys' adventure story, much in the tradition of THE MERRY ADVENTURES
OF ROBIN HOOD by Howard Pyle (the illustrations are even
similar to Pyle's, though not as detailed).

Olav is twelve years old, and wants to carry the Vikings
banner into war; it is a sign of becoming a man. The 'real'
men are off on their own adventures throughout most of the
book, but Olav meets them at the end and gets his wish.

He earns this wish to be accepted into maturity by
demonstrating his abilities at archery, swardsmanship, and the
like. War is viewed as a sport, much like football or hockey.

The setting is real, though sketchy. The characters have
the names that the Norse people of the ninth century had, and
the Norse gods are present, though not fleshed out.

080. Dehn, Paul. "Hey Diddle Diddle," p. 80, and "Little
Miss Muffet," p. 80. REFLECTIONS ON A GIFT OF WATERMELON
PICKLE . . . AND OTHER MODERN VERSE. New York: Lothrop, Lee &
Shepard, 1967. 139 pp. (ages 10-adult).

These two rewrites of standard Mother Goose rhymes offer
short, dramatic comments on nuclear war.

081. DeJong, Meindert. THE HOUSE OF SIXTY FATHERS.
Illustrated by Maurice Sendak. New York: Harper, 1956, 189 pp.
(ages 12-16).

Set in China during World War II, this story is told by
Tien Pao, a naive boy who flees upriver in a sampan with his
parents and baby sister when the Japanese invade and destroy
his village.
He meets up with Lieutenant Hamsun, an American airman,
who hires Tien to row him across the river, but this makes his
father angry because of the risk, and thus, his father takes
away the oars, resulting in Tien Pao getting washed down the
river into Japanese-held territory, where he eventually meets
up with Lieutenant Hamsun again, and experiences the take over
of Hengyang by the Japanese, finally reuniting with his
parents.
Parts of the story are hard to swallow (such as the
meetings with Lieutenant Hamsun and the "lucky" reunion with
Tien Pao's parents, but the character of Tien Pao is
believeable and likeable.

082. Dimock, Martha McHutchison. A CHRONICLE OF THE AMERICAN
REVOLUTION: 1763-1783. New York: Harper & Row, 1976, 194 pp.
(ages 14-18).

In diary format, Dimock sketches the events leading up to
and during the American Revolution. It begins by offering
brief biographies of the leaders of the revolution. Anecdotal
and easy to read, it gives the basic outline and a "feel" for
the times.

083. Dunn, Mary Lois. THE MAN IN THE BOX: A STORY FROM
VIETNAM. New York: McGraw, 1968,

Chau Li helps David Lee (which Chau Li hears as Dah Vid),
an American prisoner of the Viet Cong, escape from the same
bamboo box Chau Li's grandfather died in.
As they go through many realistically portrayed
hardships, their relationship is well-developed, and Chau Li's
character, especially, is appealing.
The hard truths of the Vietnam war are grimly put before
the reader. The plot is believable, and the reality is
honest.

084. Dunning, Stephen and Edward Lenders and Hugh Smith, ed.
REFLECTIONS ON A GIFT OF WATERMELON PICKLE . . . : AND OTHER
MODERN VERSE. Glenview, Illinois: Lothrop, Lee & Shepard,
1967, 139 pp. (ages 10-adult).

This is a marvelous collection of poems by such modern
masters as William Carlos Williams, Carl Sandberg, Theodore
Roethke, and John Ciardi, some of them, such as "War" by Dan
Roth and "Deer Hunt" by Judson Jerome, dealing with violence.

085. Eaton, Jeanette. LEADER BY DESTINY: GEORGE WASHINGTON,
MAN AND PATRIOT. Illustrated by Jack Manley Rose. New York:
Harcourt, Brace, 1938, 402 pp. (ages 12-18).

        Eaton offers a well written, human portrayal of George
Washington--better than most. Not only is his character well
fleshed out, many of those who surrounded him also take on
three-dimensions. Don't be mislead by the well done fictional
aspect--the book is firmly grounded in historical accuracy.

086. Eco, Umberto. THE BOMB AND THE GENERAL. Illustrated by
Eugenio Carmi. Translated by William Weaver. New York:
Harcourt Brace Jovanovich, 1989, 32 pp. (ages 4-6).

        An evil general wishes to start a war with atom bombs,
but he fails, and is fired. He ends up using his uniform as a
doorman, where he is rediculed. It is a simple and obvious
tale of the stupidity of war. The illustrations are fun and
creative collage collections of objects children should
recognize. However, the intent in muddled by the tone. Is
the book meant to be serious, humorous, cute, clever, what?

087. Emberley, Barbara. DRUMMER HOFF. Illustrated by Ed
Emberley. Englewood Cliffs, New Jersey: Prentice-Hall, 1967,
32 pp. (ages 3-7).

        Children love the bright colors and repetitious rhymes,
venting their zeal with squeals of excitement when the cannon
finally fires off, "Kahbahbloooom," on the second to the final
page. The continually repeated refrain, "But Drummer Hoff
fired it off," seems to suggest the firing of the cannon
(named "Sultan") is glorious event. Drummer Hoff is lucky to
be able to do it. However, a closer look shows some
disquieting elements. The man bringing the powder has a
wooden leg; the soldier packing the load into the cannon has
only one eye. The final page (sometimes removed by schools
and libraries) shows the cannon deserted in a field without
humans (perhaps the result of war).
        Ed Emberley concluded his Caldecott Award acceptance
speech:

                The book's main theme is a simple one--a group
        of happy warriors build a cannon that goes "KAH-
        BAHBLOOM." But, there is more to find if you
        "read" the pictures. They show that men can fall
        in love with war and, imitating the birds, go to
        meet it dressed as if to meet their sweethearts.
        The pictures also show that men can return from
        war sometimes with medals, and sometimes with
        wooden legs.
                The book can have two endings. Many people
        prefer to stop at the "KABAHBLOOM" page. And
        for some purposes that is where the story should
        end. But others prefer to go to the next page,
        which shows the cannon destroyed. The men have
        gone, and the birds and flowers that appear to be
        merely decorative through the first part of the
        book are in the process of taking over--again.
        The picture of the destroyed cannon was purposely

put on a half page to keep it in its proper place
as a minor theme. The main theme of the book is,
I repeat, a group of happy warriors building a
cannon that goes "KAHBAHBLOOM." The book's
primary purpose is, as it should be, to entertain.

088. Fisher, Aileen. JEANNE D'ARC. Illustrated by Ati
Forberg. New York: Crowell, 1970, 52 pp. (ages 7-10).

     This brief biography of Jeanne D'Arc strongly suggests
that she did hear voices and was able to predict the future
(at least at times). She was undoubtably brave. Whether her
bravery came from hearing the voices of angels, common sense,
or simply being crazy is hard to tell--though Aileen Fisher
and Ati Forberg apparently find her a positive role model.
     Although the illustrations (taking up a page or two pages
each) are generally well crafted in line and color, often
giving individual character to each figure's face, they
usually brake into the text in mid-sentence, interrupting the
flow.

089. Fitzhugh, Louise and Sandra Scoppetone. BANG BANG YOU'RE
DEAD. Illustrated by Louise Fitzhugh. New York: Harper & Row,
1969; Harper Trophy Edition, 1986, 32 pp. (ages 5-8).

     Two groups of boys battle for possession of a hill,
throwing rocks and hitting each other with sticks, until they
have all been badly bruised.
     The difference between "play" war and "real" war is
stressed, and the book ends with the boys deciding real war is
wrong but play war can be fun.
     The black-and-white line illustrations (with some
shading) are fairly realistic, containing blood and bruises
where appropriate, are well balanced, and extend the text.
     The book raises the question of whether or not children
can tell the difference between reality and make-believe.

090. Flinker, Moshe. YOUNG MOSHE'S DIARY: THE SPIRITUAL
TORMENT OF A JEWISH BOY IN NAZI EUROPE. Edited by Shaul Esh.
Translator anon. Jerusalem: Post Press, 1965, 126 pp. (ages
12-adult).

     Moshe Flinker and his parents were cremated in Auschwitz.
His five sisters and youngest brother survived, and when they
returned home, they found among the remains of their
belongings three notebooks Moshe kept. This interesting and
disturbing book is the edited, translated from Hebrew, version
of those notebooks. It contains an introduction by Shaul Esh
and Geoffrey Wigoder explaining Moshe's situation and life,
and briefly analyzing the faith that comes through from
Moshe's struggles.
     Undoubtably, this record of a boy's questions and
struggle to understand why God could allow such a tragedy
will bring forth similar questions from its readers.

091. Forbes, Esther. JOHNNY TREMAIN: A STORY OF BOSTON IN
REVOLT. Illustrated by Lynd Ward. Boston: Houghton Mifflin,
1943, 256 pp. (ages 12-adult).

     This is as fine an example of historical realism as
exists in children's literature. It is thoroughly researched,
the off-shoot of Ester Forbes' PAUL REVERE AND THE WORLD HE
LIVED IN, which won the 1943 Pultzer Prize for History, and it
brings the generously detailed setting of Boston at the
beginning of the American Revolution into vivid realization.
     It centers on Johnny Tremain, a talented and arrogant
apprentice in the Lapham silver shop. Since Mr. Lapham has
become nearly useless as a silver smith, Johnny has taken over
most of the work of the shop (to the distaste of the other
apprentices). One Sunday, with the help of Mrs. Lapham,
Johnny goes against the law and attempts to finish an
important silver piece commissioned by John Hancock. Dove,
one of the apprentices jealous of Johnny, purposely puts to
use a defective crucible, which breaks under the intense heat,
burning and crippling Johnny's hand; thus, ending his career
as a smith. Johnny is bitter and lost. For a while he
wanders the streets of Boston. Then he remembers his dead
mother's instructions to seek out the assistance of his rich
relative, the merchant Jonathan Lyte, if in need, and to prove
his kinship by showing him a silver cup, part of a set, that
his mother gave him before she died. Jonathan Lyte lives up
to his reputation as a dishonest, cruel man and has Johnny
imprisoned as a thief--saying that Johnny stole the cup.
     However, Rab Silsbee, who works for the Boston Observer
and who Johnny met while wandering the streets, and Cilla
Lapham, granddaughter of Johnny's former employer, prove
Johnny innocent, and Johnny accepts a job for the Boston
Observer as a currier.
     This brings Johnny directly into the center of the
revolutionary activities, since Mr. Lorne, owner of the
Observer is the Patriots' printer and the Patriots (Sam Adams,
Paul Revere, John Hancock, and James Otis) meet in the attic
where Johnny and Rab sleep
     The revolution is beginning, and Johnny is a part, though
a minor part, of it. He participates in the Boston Tea Party
and becomes a spy for the Patriots.
     Cilla and her sister, Isannah, move in to live with the
Lytes, as Lavinia, Jonathan Lyte's daughter and a woman Johnny
has longed for from a distance, has taken a liking to Isannah
and, in her spoiled manner, managed to get Isannah as
something of a protege. This results in Johnny learning his
true identity as real kin of the Lytes.
     As the fighting begins, Johnny is able to learn of the
British plans to advance on Lexington and Concord and pass
this information on to Paul Revere (who then warns the
colonists). Johnny then makes his way to Lexington to find
his friend Rab, who has set out to fight, dying. At the same
time, however, he is told that his crippled hand can be fixed
so he will be able to regain the use of it.
     The novel is a stunning presentation of the beginnings of
the struggle of the American Patriots for freedom, containing
an even-handed representation of the British soldiers (who
really were more humane towards the rowdy American Patriots
than has generally been the case in such situations throughout
history). It contains excellent character portrayal,
substantiating Ester Forbes' claim in her Newbery Acceptance

speech, 1944, for the novel, that "I would know not merely
what was done but why and how people felt." The dramatic
style keeps a complex yet compelling plot moving toward a
conclusion that is really a beginning--
the beginning of the Revolutionary War--and leaves the reader
with a surge of patriotism.
     There are twelve full page black-line drawings in a
realistic style common to children's books of the 1940s.

092. Foreman, Michael. WAR AND PEAS. Illustrated by the
author. New York: Thomas Y. Crowell, 1974, 30 pp. (ages 5-8).

     This rich, colorful, surrealistic picture book presents
King Lion, who is sad because his country has been without
rain and there is no food. He decides to ask a neighboring
country, one rich with food, for help. So he takes the
Minister of Food to the distant hills of the neighboring
kingdom. The hills are in reality (in the surrealistic sense)
hugh pieces of cake topped with cherries and other delights.
     The Fat King of that kingdom has the Lion King and his
minister seized and locked up. However, they manage to
escape. The soldiers from the Fat Kingdom are too fat to
chase them (so fat that the horses' legs spread out flat and
the truck tires burst from their weight).
     In the ensuing war, the Fat Kingdom's soldiers are easily
overcome by the Lion Kingdom's soldiers, and the food is
spread all over the place (in the manner of a huge "food
fight"). It begins to rain. Peace and plenty are at hand.
     It is debatable if children, or anyone, learns a much
from this book--though, obviously, the theme of sharing is a
part of it. There is a great deal of humor in both the
illustrations and the text, as exemplified in the final page:

               "Burrrp!" said the Fat King.
                "Peace," said the Lion.
            "No, no, no," groaned the Fat King.
              "don't mention peas, ever."
               "Peace," repeated the Lion.
            "Never heard of it," said the Fat King.
                "What's the recipe?"

093. Forman, James D. CALL BACK YESTERDAY. New York:
Scribner's, 1981, 163 pp. (ages 12-16).

     Dr. Harper, a stranger with a suspicious accent who
refuses to tell her where she is or why, draws the story out
of Cindy Cooper, the daughter of the American ambassador and
the sole survivor, as she slowly returns to consciousness
following the seizure in 1988 of the United States Embassy in
Saudi Arabia, revealing that the entire incident was a tragic
accident.
     Well drawn characters, a suspenseful technique, and the
real possibility of it happening make this an excellent novel.

094. Forman, James D. CEREMONY OF INNOCENCE. New York:
Hawthorn, 1970, 249 pp. (ages 12-16).

     In standard action-packed, tension-filled, Forman style,

this is the story of the arrest and execution of a brother and
sister for anti-Nazi underground activities.

095. Forman, James D. THE COW NECK REBELS. New York: Farrar,
Straus and Giroux, 1969, 279 pp. (ages 12-16).

     Two brothers march off to the Battle of Long Island
during the Revolutionary War and are deeply affected. Colored
maps are included.

096. Forman, James D. DOOMSDAY PLUS TWELVE. New York:
Scribner's, 1984, 230 pp. (ages 12-15).

     In the year 2,000, twelve years after a nuclear war,
Valerie, a young girl leads a peaceful crusade to prevent some
vigilantes in San Diego from taking out their frustrations
over losing it on some peaceful Japanese citizens.
     The book shows anti-war activism as a rational and
hopeful means for preventing violence (at least on the local
level), but it is overcrowded with allusions, descriptions,
and characters.

097. Forman, James D. A FINE, SOFT DAY. New York: Farrar,
Straus, and Giroux, 245 pp. (ages 12-16).

     This story presents the Belfast conflict, as a sensitive
Catholic boy and his family are drawn into it. It is one of
several excellent books on war by a masterful writer.

098. Forman, James, D. FOLLOW THE RIVER. New York: Farrar,
Straus, and Giroux, 1975, 185 pp. (ages 12-16).

     A young German, seeking a purpose in life, goes to India
to participate in a friendship walk for peace.

099. Forman, James, D. HORSES OF ANGER. Farrar, Straus, 1967,
249 pp. (ages 12-16).

     In 1944, fifteen-year-old Hans attempts to defend Munich.

100. Forman, James. MY ENEMY, MY BROTHER. Boston: Meredith
Press, 1969, 250 pp. (ages 12-adult).

     After World War II, Dan, Gideon, Sholem, and Hanna, four
young Jews who managed to survive the Holocaust, set-off for
Palestine, only to plunge into the war with the Arabs in the
Mideast.
     The book is a realistic account of the hardships and the
moral dilemmas they face, each of them responding in a
different fashion. It ends with an "Epilogue" that gives
Said's, an Arab soldier, point of view.
     Obviously, it is not a book about good guys and bad guys.
Rather, it is a book about the struggles of "good" and "evil"
within in us all--Nazis, Jews, Arabs--humans.

101. Forman, James D. PEOPLE OF THE DREAM. New York: Farrar, Straus, and Giroux, 1972, 227 pp. (ages 12-16).

This book details the four month trek of Chief Joseph and the Nez Perce from their ancestral homes to the Canadian border.

102. Forman, James D. THE SURVIVOR. New York: Farrar, Strauss & Giroux, 1976, 272 pp. (ages 12-adult).

This is a detailed account of the Ullman family's sufferings during the Holocaust, focusing on David Ullman, a teenage Jew who subsequently follows his sister to Palestine after the other members of his family die.

As with other books by James Forman, the ending is not one of resolution but one filled with new unknowns. It ends with David lying awake on the Texel Queen II, leaving Holland and heading for Palestine, and realizing that "Evil was not dead," that "Perhaps there was no God," that "The future remained a question mark."

However, as the readers know, by this point in the novel, David has gained the courage to face whatever awaits him.

103. Forman, James D. THE WHITE CROW. New York: Farrar, Strauss & Giroux, 1976, 227 pp. (ages 12-adult).

Forman offers a fictional account of Hilter's early life to his participation in the unsuccessful Putsch of November, 1923.

104. Frank, Anne. ANNE FRANK: THE DIARY OF A YOUNG GIRL. Translated by B. M. Mooyaart-Doubleday. Garden City, New York: Doubleday, 1952, 283 pp. (ages 12-adult).

This famous diary of a thirteen-year-old Jewish girl who spent two years with her family hiding from the Nazis during the occupation of Holland brings the reader into the fear and the horror of that situation. Yet it contains more than that. It contains, it expresses, what the human spirit is all about. The nobility shines through the darkness.

In the "Introduction," Eleanor Roosevelt writes:

> These are the thoughts and expression of a young girl living under extraordinary conditions, and for this reason her diary tells us much about our-selves and about our own children. And for this reason, too, I felt how close we all are to Anne's experience, how very much involved we are in her short life and in the entire world.
>
> Anne's diary is an appropriate monument to her fine spirit and to the spirits of those who have worked and are working still for peace. Reading it is a rich and rewarding experience.

The sad nobility of the diary is heightened by the realization that Anne Frank died in the Bergen-Belsen concentration camp in March of 1945, only two months before the liberation of Holland.

105. Freedman, Russell. LINCOLN: A PHOTOBIOGRAPHY. New York:
Houghton Mifflin, 1987, 150 pp. (ages 10-adult).

    This well written winner of the 1988 Newbery Award
captures the personality of Lincoln (his gift for
storytelling, his embarrassment over his lack of culture, and
his strong desire to succeed), and the complexity of his
presidency, (his constant struggles with political, military,
ethical, practical, and personal demands)--all tied to the
question of slavery and the desire to keep the country intact,
and leads the reader to the touching final chapter, where, the
book reminds us (or shows some of us for the first time) why
we admire this man. His assassination is presented in a
simple, human way--bound to bring a frustrated "Why?" to the
thoughts of the reader (Why do great men have to be killed?).
Of course, there is a real sense that Lincoln had, indeed,
finished his task. It would be hard to ask more of him.
    The collection of black-and-white prints is excellent,
and the text includes a sampling of Lincoln's more famous
sayings, a list of important Lincoln memorials, monuments, and
museums, and a brief discussion of some of the better books
out about him.

106. Friesel, Uwe. TIM, THE PEACEMAKER. Illustrated by Jozef
Wilkon. New York: Scroll Press, 1971, 24 pp. (ages 4-8).

    Tim plays the flute so well that all who hear him stop
whatever they are doing to listen, so much so that they even
forget to eat and thus grow thin. This makes Tim sad.
However, he then plays his flute in front of an army marching
to war, and they all forget about war and get so wrapped up in
the music that they even make their own flutes. This makes
Tim happy.
    It is a simple story for younger children, a fantasy
where music overcomes the desire to fight. The illustrations
by Jozef Wilkon are well done.

107. Fritz, Jean. AND THEN WHAT HAPPENED, PAUL REVERE?
Illustrated by Margot Tomes. New York: Coward, McCann and
Geoghegan, 1973, 48 pp. (ages 7-10).

    As always, Jean Fritz has brought her historical
character to life, in this case offering a picture of Paul
Revere as a forgetful dreamer who went on his famous ride in
such a hurry that he left his door open, a fortunate
occurence, since it allowed his dog to bring him the spurs he
also forgot.
    Jean Fritz's books dealing with American History for
younger children are always humorous, well-informed narratives
illustrated by highly respected children's illustrators.
Other important titles, along with some books for older youth,
follow.

108. Fritz, Jean. BRADY. Illustrated by Lynd Ward. New York:
Coward, McCann and Geoghegan, 1960, 223 pp. (ages 10-14).

This is a lively portrayal of the roots of the Civil War. Once again, as always with Jean Fritz, setting and historical accuracy are excellent. The moral issues of the Abolitionist view are also considered.

109. Fritz, Jean. CAN'T YOU MAKE THEM BEHAVE, KING GEORGE? Illustrated by Tomie de Paola. New York: Coward, McCann and Geoghegan, 1977, 45 pp. (ages 8-10).

This humorous portrait of King George is not as enjoyable as those of the founding fathers, but contains the same easily understood historical data.

110. Fritz, Jean. CAST FOR A REVOLUTION: SOME AMERICAN FRIENDS AND ENEMIES, 1728-1814. Boston: Houghton, Mifflin, 1972, 400 pp. (15-adult).

This book for older youth and adults offers a thorough background of scholarship on the Revolutionary War. Jean Fritz calls it a collective biography. It gives insights into such important Founding Fathers and Mothers as James Otis, James Warren and his wife Mercy Warren, Sam Adams, and John Hancock.
It is a more serious book, aimed at a much older audience than Fritz' numerous picture books on the subject for young children.

111. Fritz, Jean. EARLY THUNDER. Illustrated by Lynd Ward. New York: Coward, McCann and Geoghegan, 1967, 255 pp. (ages 10-16).

Based on "real events beginning with Judge Ropes' death, including the two sessions of the General Court, the town meeting of August 24th, the fire of October 5th, and ending with the Affair at North Bridge on February 26th which was in reality, although no shorts were fired, the first confrontation in the Revolutionary War," this novel presents the reader with Daniel West (a fictional character), who lives in Salem, Massachusetts, in 1775.
In the beginning, Daniel was a devoted Tory who hated the Liberty Boys and the Whig-Tory conflict that was tearing apart Salem (and the rest of the new world).
As time went on, however, Daniel's loyalities became mixed, and finally, he was forced to face his beliefs head on.
The book is a skillful piece of historical fiction, revealing the human struggle many revolutionary Americans encountered at the start of the revolt.
The few detailed black-and-white illustrations in a realistic style go well with the text.

112. Fritz, Jean. GEORGE WASHINGTON'S BREAKFAST. Illustrated by Paul Galdone. New York: Coward, McCann and Geoghegan, 1969, (ages 8-10).

113. Fritz, Jean. MAKE WAY FOR SAM HOUSTON. Illustrated by Elise Primavera. New York: Putnam, 1986, 109 pp. (ages 10-13).

Yet again, Jean Fritz manages to bring a legend to life (warts and all). Though he had too much pride, a drinking problem, and a bad temper, Sam Houston, as Jean Fritz indicates, was also filled with vision, energy and patriotism.

114. Fritz, Jean. SHH: WE'RE WRITING THE CONSTITUTION. Illustrated by Tomie de Paola. New York: Putnam, 1987, 64 pp. (ages 7-10).

Filling the story with often humorous details, Jean Fritz offers a brief (perhaps, in this case, too brief) report of the writing of the constitution.

115. Fritz, Jean. STONEWALL. Illustrated by Stephen Gammell. New York: Putnam, 1979, 152 pp. (ages 7-10).

This is a skillful depiction of a powerful, obsessed Thomas Jonathan Jackson--one of the more unusual of the American heroes.

116. Fritz, Jean. TRAITOR: THE CASE OF BENEDICT ARNOLD. Illustrated by John Andre. New York: Putnam, 1981, 191 pp. (ages 7-10).

This is a non-judgemental picture of probably the most famous traitor in America's history. As always, Jean Fritz has filled it with facts.

117. Fritz, Jean. WHAT'S THE BIG IDEA, BEN FRANKLIN? Illustrated by Margot Tomes. New York: Coward, McCann and Geoghegan, 1976, 48 pp. (ages 6-8).

As always, Jean Fritz has filled her book with details and accurate historical data, quickly revealing the many interests of another of the country's founding fathers.

118. Fritz, Jean. WHERE WAS PATRICK HENRY ON THE 29TH OF MAY? Illustrated by Margot Tomes. New York: Putnam, 1982, 48 pp. (ages 8-10).

Once again, Jean Fritz offers a humorous telling of some of the major incidents and important traits of one of the important leaders of Revolutionary War.

119. Fritz, Jean. WHY DON'T YOU GET A HORSE, SAM ADAMS? Illustrated by Trina S. Hyman. New York: Coward, McCann and Geoghegan, 1974, 47 pp. (ages 7-10).

Sam Adams is pictured as a man who is totally absorbed by the Revolutionary War.

120. Fritz, Jean. WILL YOU SIGN HERE, JOHN HANCOCK? Illustrated by Trina S. Hyman. New York: Coward, McCann and Geoghegan, 1976, 47 pp. (ages 7-10).

John Hancock is pictured as a friendly, well liked, man--though a bit vain and overly desirous of comfort and luxury.

121.   Gardam, Jane. A LONG WAY FROM VERONA. New York: Macmillan, 1971, 190 pp. (ages 12-adult).

Thirteen-year-old Jessica, a young girl aspiring to be a writer, recounts her experiences growing up in England during World War II. The book is a well written combination of the dark terrors and the humor of the war.

122.   Garfield, Leon. THE DRUMMER BOY. New York: Pantheon, 1969, 185 pp. (ages 11-15).

After their regiment's defeat in France (10,000 men are killed), a drummer boy and six other survivors struggle back to England and an uncertain future. The drummer boy delivers a message to the General's daughter from her dead soldier/ lover and falls in love with her himself, later discovering that both the general and his daughter have sick minds. The drummer boy finally follows a surgeon (who reveals true courage and compassion) and finds true love in Charity, the General's daughter's maid.
It is well written, containing both the horrors of war and a good deal of humor.

123.   Gauch, Patricia Lee. THIS TIME, TEMPE WICK? Illustrated by Margot Tomes. New York: Coward, McCann and Geoghegan, 1974, 43 pp. (ages 6-9).

Patricia Lee Gauch recounts the adventures of Temperance Wick, a colonial girl, who, legend has it, stood up to some not-so-wholesome American Revolutionary soldiers to keep them from stealing her horse.
The illustrations are by Margot Tomes, famous for illustrating such children's classics as Jean Fritz's AND THEN WHAT HAPPENED, PAUL REVERE?

124.   Gehrts, Barbara. DON'T SAY A WORD. Translated by Elizabeth D. Crawford. New York: McElderry, 1986, 169 pp. (ages 12-adult).

Yet another of the many excellent books for teenagers written by one who experienced the terrors first hand, this fictionalized memoir, written in the first person by Anna Singelmann, presents an adolescent's rapid maturation and understanding of the horrible truths of the reign of Hitler.

125.   Gibran, Kahlil. "Peace," TEARS AND LAUGHTER. Translated by Anthony Rizcallah Ferris. Edited by Martin L. Wolf. New York: The Wisdom Library, 1949, 2 pp. (ages 14-adult).

This poem by the highly regarded Lebanonese poet-philosopher, in standard Gibran poetic language, filled with metaphors of nature and personification of abstract

qualities, pictures the return of a young man from war and his
reunion with the woman who suffered in fear of his death. It
ends:

> At dawn the two stood in the middle of the
> field, contemplating the beauty of Nature injured
> by the tempest. After a deep and comforting
> silence, the soldier looked to the east and said
> to his sweetheart, "Look at the Darkness, giving
> birth to the Sun."

126. Ginsburg, Marvell. THE TATTOOED TORAH. Illustrated by Jo
Gershman. New York: Union of American Hebrew Congregations,
1983, 28 pp. (ages 4-8).

This is based on a true story of the discovery and
restoration of the Brno Torah and is meant to introduce young
children to the Jewish heritage and the tragedy of the
holocaust. It must be meant to be read to or with children,
for many aspects of it (both the Jewish terms and the
Holocaust) will need explaining, especially to non-Jewish
children.
The story is narrated partially by the "little torah,"
somewhat in the manner of a young child, which may work for
younger children, but has a very "cute" feel about it,
especially when juxtaposed with the horror it is telling
about.
The illustrations in orange and black do extend the text
(once again containing many things that would need explaining
to younger children and most non-Jewish people). They are
cartoonish in character, perhaps more attractive for young
children but not fitting well with the subject matter.

127. Glenn, Mel. CLASS DISMISSED! Photographs by Michael J.
Bernstein. New York: Clarion Books, 1982, 96 pp. (ages
10-adult).

This is a collection of poems written by a high school
English teacher meant to capture the hopes and fears of
students he has known. It contains "Song Vu Chin," a good
poem supposedly written by a Vietnamese immigrant about the
war in Vietnam. The style of the poem is similar to Bob
Dylan's "A Hard Rain's a Gonna Fall."

128. Golding, William. LORD OF THE FLIES. Biographical and
Critical Notes by E. L. Epstein. New York: Putnam, 1954, 192
pp. (ages 14-adult).

This outstanding first novel by William Golding depicts
the rapid degeneration of a group of English boys who are
stranded on an island during World War II, and can be read on
several levels.
On one level it is a boys' adventure story, filled with
the excitement and action of surviving in the wilderness. On
another level it is a metaphysical drama about evil and good
(The Lord of the Flies is a phrase for the Devil). On another
level, a psychological level, the Lord of the Flies is the Id
(the anarchic, amoral, driving energy within us all), and the

events of the story represent the rapid succumbing to this inner force of a normal group of boys when they are given a chance to control their own destiny. On yet another level, it is a commentary on the current world situation and civili- zation in general. After all, the adults who rescue Ralph belong to a cruiser involved in an adult war.

At the center of it all is a dark commentary on basic human nature; the entire novel radiates out from the following scene where Simon encounters The Beast:

> "You are a silly little boy," said the Lord of the Flies, "just an ignorant, silly little boy."
> Simon moved his swollen tongue but said nothing.
> "Don't you agree?" said the Lord of the Flies. "Aren't you just a silly little boy?"
> Simon answered him in the same silent voice.
> "Well then," said the Lord of the Flies, "you'd better run off and play with the others. They think you're batty. You don't want Ralph to think you're batty, do you? You like Ralph a lot, don't you? And Piggy, and Jack?"
> Simon's head was tilted slightly up. His eyes could not break away and the Lord of the Flies hung in space before him.
> "What are you doing out here all alone? Aren't you afraid of me?"
> Simon shook.
> "There isn't anyone to help you. Only me. And I'm the Beast."
> Simon's mouth labored, brought forth audible words.
> "Pig's head on a stick."
> "Fancy thinking the Beast was something you could hunt and kill!" said the head. For a moment or two the forest and all the other dimly appreciated places echoes with the parody of laughter. "You knew, didn't you? I'm part of you? Close, close, close! I'm the reason why it's no go? Why things are what they are?"
> The laughter shivered again. [pp. 132-33]

At the end of this scene, Simon looks into "a vast mouth" with a "blackness within, a blackness that spread," a symbolic representation of "ravenous, unreasoning and eternally insatiable nature," as E. L. Epstein correctly points out in his commentary, and as he also points out, a symbol that lies at the center of Joseph Conrad's HEART OF DARKNESS.

The darkness within us all--that is subject of the novel.

Is it any wonder that this highly acclaimed novel, often included in secondary school curriculums, is also highly controversial?

129. Goldston, Robert. THE CIVIL WAR IN SPAIN. Illustrated by Donald Carrick. New York: Bobbs-Merrill, 1967, 224 pp. (ages 14-adult).

After a brief outline of Spanish history up to 1939, Goldston offers a detailed chronology of the war from 1939 to

1942. It is a clearly presented picture of a tragic event
that drew the lines for much modern ideology. It includes an
impressive index and bibliography.
     Goldston has written several similar books on important
events in recent history, some of which are listed below.

130.   Goldston, Robert. THE LIFE AND DEATH OF NAZI GERMANY.
Illustrations and Photography by Donald Carrick. New York:
Bobbs-Merrill, 1967, 224 pp. (ages 14-adult).

     This is a straight-forward history aimed at teenagers.
It includes a bibliography, index, maps, photographs, and
drawings.
     The final chapter assesses the German people's
responsibility for the Nazi atrocities and sounds a warning
against possible future wars.

131.   Goldston, Robert. THE RISE OF CHINA. Illustrated by
Donald Carrick. New York: Bobbs-Merrill, 1967, 256 pp. (ages
14-adult).

     This is a standard history, this time of the Social
Revolution that took place in China in the twentieth century.

132.   Goldston, Robert. THE RUSSIAN REVOLUTION. Illustrated by
Donald Carrick. New York: Bobbs-Merrill, 1967, 224 pp. (ages
14-adult).

     Once again, a well researched history, this one deals
with the Russian Revolution.

133.   Goode, Michael. "Addition Problem," THE VOICE OF THE
CHILDREN. Edited by June Jordan and Terri Bush. New York:
Holt, Rinehart & Winston, 1970, 101 pp. (ages 8-adult).

     Michael Goode, age thirteen, lines up words, such as
mother, father, friends, enemies, hell, and heaven, in the
form of an addition problem which adds up to war.

134.   Gordon, George. (See Lord Byron).

135.   Graham, Gail. CROSS-FIRE: A VIETNAM NOVEL. Illustrated
by David Stone Martin. New York: Pantheon, 1972, 135 pp. (ages
12-adult).

     Harry, a young American soldier, gets separated from his
unit and joins up with four Vietnamese children, survivors of
a village that has been destroyed by American bombs. As they
travel through the Vietnamese jungle, facing tough challenges
(the baby Vietnamese child dies in the process), they help one
another survive--though never completely overcoming their
distrust of one another.
     The cold, unstopable destruction of war surrounds them,
eventually resulting in Harry's death. The style is blunt and
realistic, though there are flaws (i.e., B-52s simply do not

stalk a lone individual on the ground, as this novel presents
it).

136.   Graves, Robert. THE SIEGE AND FALL OF TROY. Illustrated
by C. Walter Hodges. New York: Doubleday, 1962, 128 pp. (ages
8-12).

   Robert Graves, a noted expert on Greek and Roman
mythology, presents a simplified prose version of the fall of
Troy (including the journey of Odysseus), revealing all the
common human characteristics that accompany war--greed,
avarice, stupidity, pain. It is a good introduction to the
Trojan War.

137.   Green, Diana Huss. THE LONELY WAR OF WILLIAM PINTO.
Boston: Little, Brown, 1968, 171 pp. (ages 10-adult).

   Basing the story on a real Jewish family, whose two older
sons joined the American Revolution early on and whose younger
son, William Pinto did not, until near the end, Diana Huss
Green has written a novel dealing with a seldom considered
aspect of the Revolutionary War, the response of the Jewish
community and the prejudice against anti-Semitism during that
time.

138.   Greene, Bette. SUMMER OF MY GERMAN SOLDIER. New York:
Dial Press, 1974, 230 pp. (ages 13-adult).

   Patty Ann Bergern, a twelve-year-old Jewish girl, helps a
German POW escape from an Arkansas prison camp during World
War II. He gets shot and killed. She gets rejected by her
family and put in reform school. The only one who understands
is Ruth, the family's maid (who is similar to Maime Trotter in
Katherine Paterson's THE GREAT GILLY HOPKINS).
   Taking an interesting reverse angle on the subject, this
is an excellent story about the horrors of blind prejudice and
the nobility of standing up to it (in spite of the necessary
suffering for so doing). It will bring tears to the eyes of
sensitive readers.

139.   Gregory, Horace and Marya Zaturenska, ed. THE CRYSTAL
CABINET: AN INVITATION TO POETRY. Wood engravings by Diana
Bloomfield. New York: Holt, Rinehart and Winston, 1962, 225
pp. (ages 10-adult).

   Named after a William Blake poem (and the first poem
included in the collection), this is an excellent gathering of
some of the greatest poems ever written, including a section
titled "We Were the Heroes," which has such poems as Archibald
MacLeish's "The Silent Slain" and Horace Gregory's "Voices of
Heroes."

140.   Gurko, Leo.   TOM PAINE: FREEDOM'S APOSTLE. Illustrated
by Fritz Kredel. New York: Thomas Y. Crowell, 1957, 213 pp.
(ages 12-16).

Leo Gurko, after thoroughly researching Tom Paine with the help of a grant from the Ford Foundation, has brought to life this complex writer who stirred the minds of the American Revolutionaries, presenting both the weaknesses (e.g., Paine was a failure at business, indiscreet, and disliked by many) and the brilliant, uncompromising idealist.

The biography begins with Paine's arrival in the United States at age thirty-seven and follows his life through to his death at age seventy-two, raising the issues, the questions, the rightness and/or wrongness of revolution and war.

The simple line drawings at the beginning of each chapter by Fritz Kredel, while not outstanding, do extend the text and add to the value of the book.

141. Habenstreit, Barbara. MEN AGAINST WAR. Garden City, New York: Doubleday, 1973, 210 pp. (ages 12-adult).

Barbara Habenstreit presents a good history of pacifism in the United States, from the Shakers refusal to fight against Chief Tecumseh in the first part of the nineteenth century to the anti-war movement during the late 1960s.

A brief list of "Suggested Reading" offers additional books on the subject.

This well written book is more detailed than a similar excellent book, AIN'T GONNA STUDY WAR NO MORE, by Melvin Meltzer, and offers an energetic, even-handed view of a much needed perspective to go along with the typical pro-war history books generally used in schools.

142. Halliday, E. M. RUSSIA IN REVOLUTION. Cyril E. Black, consultant. New York: Harper and Row, 1967, 153 pp. (ages 12-adult).

This is one of a series of Horizon Caravel Books dealing with important events in history, in this case the Russian Revolution. It contains an index and a list of books for further reading, as well as numerous photographs in black-and-white and a few illustrations in color.

The book has been thoroughly researched, and the events leading up to, including, and following the revolution are presented in a straight forward manner. While pointing out the inevitability of the revolution, the book also states that the actual revolution came about in an unexpected, unplanned manner. In face, in the second week of March, when the striking workers in Petrograd really began the revolution, the major leaders behind it were in other parts of the world. Lenin was in Switzerland. Trotsky was in New York, and Stalin was in Siberia. None of them expected the violent rebellion that took place.

The revolution is followed through to Lenin's death, and a few added pages are offered summing up Lenin the man.

The analysis and evaluation of the revolution and the men behind it is even handed and offers a good beginning to an understanding of the background of the contemporary situation in the Soviet Union.

143.   Hardy, Thomas. "The Man He Killed"; rpt., p. 117,
CAVALCADE OF POEMS. Edited by George Bennett and Paul Molloy.
New York: Scholastic, 1968, 120 pp. (ages 10-adult).

      This is a simply put reflection on meeting a man in war
and shooting him, though, in other circumstances, he might
well be a good friend. It's matter-of-fact approach provides
a starkly realistic truth.
      Thomas Hardy, 1840-1928, is best known for his darkly
pessimistic novels, but also produced a large body of poetry,
and an epic verse drama, THE DYNASTS, based on the Napoleonic
Wars--all for adults.
      Another poem of his on war often included in collections
of poetry is "In Time of 'The Breaking of Nations,'" a short
three verse statement on the continuing of the simpler,
natural activities of life long after war's interruptions have
been forgotten.

144.   Harrison, Deloris, ed. WE SHALL LIVE IN PEACE: THE
TEACHINGS OF MARTIN LUTHER KING, JR. Illustrated by Ernest
Crichlow. New York: Hawthorn Books, 1968, 64 pp. (ages 8-12).

      This is a nice introduction to the 1964 winner of the
Nobel Prize for Peace. It has fewer illustrations than either
Margaret B. Young's or Nigel Hunter's similar books, but the
quality of Crichlow's drawings is far superior--as is
Harrison's writing.

145.   Haskins, James. RESISTANCE: PROFILES IN NONVIOLENCE. New
York: Doubleday, 1970, 164 pp. (ages 10-adult).

      After giving a brief introductory discussion of
non-violence, the ten "Bench Marks" or rules of non-violence,
and definitions of important terms, James Haskins offers brief
biographies of famous pacifists, including Jesus, Gandhi,
Martin Luther King, Jr., and Bertrand Russell.
      It is a good introduction to a pacifist viewpoint.
Readers may wish to continue reading on the subject by turning
to Barbara Habenstreit, MEN AGAINST WAR, and Melvin Meltzer,
AIN'T GONNA STUDY WAR NO MORE.

146.   Haugaard, Erik Christian. THE LITTLE FISHES. Illustrated
by Milton Johnson. Gloucester, Mass.: Peter Smith, 1986, 214
pp. (ages 10-adult).

      Erik Christian Haugaard prefaces the story by saying he
wrote it in response to questions from children who ask
veterans "What was it [World War II] like?" And the story he
has written is the story of three children (Guido, who tells
the story, Anna, and Mario, who dies), their begging in
Naples, and their journey from Naples to Cassino in 1943.
      But that is mere plot. The story is much more. It has a
wonderful quality of parable about it (though it isn't a
parable), and the sense of myth (though it is a very
realistically detailed picture of poor children, beggars, in
Italy, struggling just to find enough to eat). The comparison
of the children to little fishes is first stated by a German
soldier:

"In the unclean waters live the little fishes.
Some are eaten; most, I believe. But some will
escape."

Guido and Anna do survive, but face an uncertain future.
In the "Epilogue" the author states:

I like to think that Anna and Guido did well, that
they became happy. . . . Yet a kind wish is like a
summer cloud, it brings no rain to the parched
earth.

I highly recommend this book. It has real characters,
who steal and beg and cheat, as well as share and hurt and
honestly care for one another. The setting is fully realized,
and the themes are eternal.

147. Hauptly, Denis J. IN VIETNAM. New York: Atheneum, 1985,
174 pp. (ages 12-adult).

Denis J. Hauptly places the United States involvement in
Vietnam in the larger context of Vietnam's history and the
difficult questions surrounding the reasons and politics and
morality of the war, offering a good, factual introduction to
the history of Vietnam. Several black-and-white photographs
and maps are included.

148. Hautzig, Esther. THE ENDLESS STEPPE. New York: Crowell,
1968, 243 pp. (ages 12-16).

A fictionalized biography of the exile of Jews from
Poland to Siberia just before the Nazi invasion, it begins in
1941, when Esther and her family, Polish Jews of great wealth
and prestige, are herded into a cattle car and transported
from their home in Vilna to the wooded barracks of a frontier
village in Siberia.
The writing is free of the bitterness and hate often
accompanying such books, and it is filled with courage, love,
affection, and even humor, as the family struggles to survive
the daily hardships. Beneath this struggle lies a great
reservoir of the deepest and most poignant emotions.

149. Hemens, Felicia. "Casabianca," 1839; rpt., p. 159, THE
GOLDEN TREASURY OF POETRY. Illustrated by Joan Walsh Anglund.
Edited by Louis Untermeyer. New York: Golden Press, 1959, 324
pp. (all ages).

The poem relates the death of a brave or simply ignorant
young boy at the Battle of the Nile between Napoleon's French
forces and the British fleet under the command of Admiral
Nelson, August 1, 1798.

150. Hersey, John. HIROSHIMA. New York: Bantam, 1984, ages
12-adult).

This journalistic masterpiece follows the lives of six
survivors of the atomic explosion over Hiroshima, revealing

the human side of both the Japanese (who were often depicted
as inhuman creatures during World War II) and the tragic
result of a nuclear explosion over a populated city. Whether
or not Little Boy (the name of the atomic bomb) should have
been dropped and can be justified for various reasons (which
sometimes include the theory that it saved more lives than
were killed in the explosion by shortening the war), any
sensitive person reading this book must face the terrible
consequences of it.

It is "the" book to read about Hiroshima. Then, for an
even more detailed account from a Japanese writer, older youth
should read BLACK RAIN by Misuji Ibuse.

151. Heyman, Eva. THE DIARY OF EVA HEYMAN. Translated by
Moshe M. Kohn. Yad Vashem, Jerusalem: Alpha Press, 1974, pp.
(ages 12-adult).

Eva Heyman was a thirteen-year-old Hungarian Jew deported
to Auschwitz, where she died. This is a diary keep from her
birthday until three months later, just before she was picked
up, and it gives her thoughts and feelings of the situation in
Hungary in 1944.

152. Hill, Douglas. THE HUNTSMANS, 1982, 132 pp.; WARRIORS OF
THE WASTELAND, 1983, 130 pp.; ALIEN CITADEL, 1984, 124 pp. A
trilogy. New York: Atheneum. (ages 12-15).

Aliens, the Slavers, invade Earth, and the humans
liberate themselves through a ruthless, savage violence--
suggesting, in spite of the book's conclusion asking for peace
and harmony, that violence is the only way to survive.

153. Hoehling, Mary. GIRL SOLDIER AND SPY: SARAH EMMA
EDMUNDSON. New York: Julian Messner, 1959, 192 pp. (ages
10-adult).

This is a well researched biography of Sarah Emma
Edmundson, a Canadian who disguises herself as a man to join
the Union Army during the Civil War (reminding one of Peter,
Paul and Mary singing "Cruel War"). The book's "Prologue"
points out that women at that time "had no more civil rights
than the Negro slaves." However, "dressed in men's clothing,
they shouldered guns and marched beside their brothers. Many
died for the Union they loved. With an army blanket their
only coffin, they were put to rest, nameless in a soldier's
grave."

Sarah did not die, but lived to tell of her experiences
and was eventually honored with membership in the Grand Army
of the Republic.

The book is well researched and written, and has both a
bibliography and an index. It is a story both of war and
women's equality--a good read for teenagers.

Another good book offering a Canadian perspective on the
Civil War aimed at a similar audience is Janet Lunn's ROOT
CELLAR.

154. Hoehling, Mary. THADDEUS LOWE: AMERICA'S ONE-MAN AIR
CORPS. New York: Julian Messner, 1958, 189 pp. (Ages
10-adult).

When you think about the soldiers fighting in the Civil
War, men lined up in fields carrying muskets with bayonets
attached, cannons that had to be dragged into position by
horse so they could fire large balls into the enemy, cavalry
charges, tents--do you ever include hot air balloons?
This is a well written account of Thaddeus Lowe, the man
who developed the inflated balloon and lead the aeronautic
corps (developed as a result of his efforts) into battle in
the Civil War. It is thoroughly researched and includes an
excellent bibliography and even some rare photographs from the
Smithsonian Institute.

155. Hogan, Jan. GLADDYS MAKES PEACE. Illustrated by Jeanine
Wine. Elgin, IL: Brethren Press, 1985, 27 pp. (ages 3-6).

This is a short picture book in verse about Gladdys Ester
Muir (1895-1967), founder of the Peace Studies Institute at
Manchester College, the first program of its kind, and a life
time crusader for peace. It is meant for pre-school or early
school children.
It mentions how she liked to sing and read and bake pie,
and how she taught history and served tea to her students when
she grew up. It ends with her holding a sign that reads "No
Bombs."
The illustrations in color, though not among those of the
top quality children's illustrators of today, help get across
the message and do extend the text.

156. Hollander, John and Harold Bloom. THE WIND AND THE RAIN:
AN ANTHOLOGY OF POEMS FOR YOUNG PEOPLE. Garden City, New York:
Doubleday, 1961, 264 pp. (all ages).

Several poems on war and killing, including "Soldier's
Song" by Tobias Hume (which praises war) and "Jesse James," an
anonymous narrative of his violent life and death, are included in this eclectic collection of poems loosely organized
around the four seasons.

157. Holm, Anne. NORTH TO FREEDOM. Translated by L. W.
Kingsland. New York: Harcourt Brace Jovanovich, 1965, 190 pp.
(ages 11-adult).

Twelve-year-old David knows only the honor of the
concentration camp. Then, for reasons David cannot understand, his hated Nazi guard arranges for him to escape, and
plans a route for him to Denmark. While David journeys
physically, a far more exciting psychological journey takes
place--the passage from a frightened, perhaps insane child,
who knows little of the real world, back to sanity.
Though there are obvious differences in style, the book
has similarities to Robert Cormier's I AM THE CHEESE. Both
books subtly reveal the horrible logic of war and the
tremendous harm it can cause an innocent individual (who, to
use a cliche, is a mere pawn in its mad logic), by following a

child's inner search to recover a past that was cruelly taken
from him.
     At times, what David knows and his ability to "suddenly"
figure things out, demand a suspension of disbelief (more so
than in I AM THE CHEESE), but the poetic quality of the
messages makes that suspension a worthwhile one.

158. Holmes, Oliver Wendell. "Grandmother's Story of Bunker
Hill Battle," COMPLETE POETICAL WORDS, 1895; rpt., pp.
178-182, THE GOLDEN TREASURY OF POETRY. Edited by Louis
Untermeyer. Illustrated by Joan Walsh Anglund. New York:
Golden Press, 1959, 324 pp. (all ages).

     A grandmother gives a lively account of the Battle of
Bunker Hill, June 17, 1755. The rhythm and the humor and the
vibrant manner of the telling make it all seem a great
adventure.

159. Howard, Vanessa. "The Last Riot," THE VOICE OF THE
CHILDREN. Ed. June Jordan and Terri Bush. New York: Rinehart
and Winston, 1970, 103 pp. (ages 10-18).

     Vanessa Howard, age thirteen, tells of the atrocities and
pain of war and offers the belief that all wars would end if
people would be thoughtful to one another, especially people
of different races.

160. Huie, William Bradford. HIROSHIMA PILOT. New York:
Putnam, 1964; New York: Pocket, 1965, 344 pp. (ages 14-adult).

     This is a gripping non-fiction account of Major Claude
Eatherly, who commanded Straight Flush, which made a simulated
bomb run over Hiroshima to test for visibility and then
radioed an all-clear signal to the Enola Gay to fly over and
drop the first atomic bomb.
     After that experience, Claude Eatherly twice attempted
suicide, committed a series of bizarre crimes, and was the
subject of sanity hearings in Waco, Texas.
     He came to stand for anti-bomb positions and was eulo-
gized as a martyr by anti-nuclear groups. He was a living
representation of the assuming of personal responsibility for
carrying out orders in the role of a soldier.

161. Hume, Ruth Fox. FLORENCE NIGHTINGALE. Illustrated by
Robert Frankenberg. New York: Random House, 1960, 184 pp.
(ages 10-14).

     Ruth Fox Hume often quotes from Florence Nightingale's
own writings as she presents a fast moving biography of
Florence Nightingale's remarkable accomplishments in bringing
medical aid to the victims of war.
     The two-color illustrations by Robert Frankenberg are
acceptable but not outstanding.

162. Hunt, Irene. ACROSS FIVE APRILS. New York: Follett,
1964, 223 pp. (ages 12-adult).

Irene Hunt, a highly respected children's writer, offers here the story of the Creighton family, who live in southern Illinois during the Civil War. With detailed descriptions and accurate dialogue, she brings the characters to life and presents many of the shades between good and bad, right and wrong.

She states in an "Author's Note" that in addition to her research, she got much of the story from stories told by her grandfather (she says that the story really is his story and dedicates the book to his great-grandchildren).

163. Hunter, Nigel. MARTIN LUTHER KING, JR. Illustrated by Richard Hook. New York: Bookwright Press, 1985, 32 pp. (ages 6-10).

One of the "Great Lifes" series, the brief photobiography of Martin Luther King, Jr., contains black-and-white and color photographs and drawings, and lists of important dates, new words, and books to read.

It is aimed at a slightly older audience than Margaret B. Young's biography of King.

164. Ibuse, Misuji. BLACK RAIN. Translated by John Bester. New York: Bantam, 1985, 300 pp. (ages 14-adult).

Misuji Ibuse is considered one of Japan's greatest twentieth century writers, and was awarded both Japan's Cultural Medal and Noma Prize (the highest literary award in Japan).

This book, based on real diaries and interviews with survivors, depicts the tragic life following the atomic explosion over Hiroshima in brutal, unflinching detail, mainly following Yasuko (a Japanese businessman) as he attempts to flesh out a diary of the incident. While the horrors are graphically related and the dark disillusionment of the experience comes through, the amazing resilience and affirmation of life (and even a keen sense of humor) are bound to leave the reader with a fuller, deeper appreciation of the human condition.

This is an excellent book for mature youth and adults and should be read in conjunction with John Hersey's HIROSHIMA.

165. Innocenti, Roberto. ROSE BLANCHE. Translated by Martha Coventry and Richard Graglia. Mankato, Minnesota: Creative Education, 1985, 32 pp. (ages 8-adult).

This excellent but highly controversial picture book offers one non-Jewish girl's experience of the incarceration of the Jews during World War II. Roberto Innocenti states, in the inside cover flap:

> In this book I wanted to illustrate how a child experiences war without really understanding it. After drawing the first page I chose Rose Blanche as its title, because of the significance of the name. "Rose Blanche" was a group of young German citizens protesting the war. They had understood what others wanted to ignore. They

were all killed.
      In this book fascism is a day-to-day reality.
Only the victims and the little girl have known
its real face.

      Roberto Innocenti was a young child growing up in Bagno a
Rapoli, a small near Florence, when the war "passed in front
of my door." The setting of this book might well be very
similar to what he experienced. Rose Blanche watches the take
over of her town by the Nazis through her window, eventually
walks out of town, follows the tracks of the trucks that have
been taking other children away, and comes to an electric
barbed wire fence. Other children stand in front of long
wooden houses, caged in by the fence. They are hungry. Rose
gives them some bread. She brings them more food during
following weeks and months. They continue to grow thinner.
      Then people begin fleeing the town and Rose Blanche
disappears. She has walked toward the barbed wire fence. But
this time she finds the camp is torn down. Shadows are moving
through the fog. The is a shot.
      New soldiers come into the town. Spring arrives. Rose
Blanche's mother waits for Rose, but Rose does not return.
      This is a beautifully illustrated picture book with large
color illustrations (mostly in browns and grays) on each page,
some covering two pages. The realistic details are excellent,
and the illustrations alone could carry the story and tragic
themes of the Holocaust. But the words are also well written
and express in simple language the same sad truths we must
learn from the tragedy they depict. These are harsh truths
about what humans are capable of, and they are presented in a
straightforward manner.
      This hard, honest treatment has adults wondering about
the audience for the book. It is a picture book, but perhaps
it is a picture book for adults. However, I have witnessed a
seventh grade class discuss it intelligently. Whatever the
audience, it is an excellent book.
      Some other picture books that also deal with war in a
harsh manner include THE BUTTER BATTLE BOOK by Dr. Seuss,
HIROSHIMA NO PIKA by Toshi Maruki and THE TIN-POT FOREIGN
GENERAL AND THE OLD IRON WOMAN and WHEN THE WIND BLOWS both by
Raymond Briggs.

166.   Japanese Broadcasting Corporation, ed. UNFORGETTABLE
FIRE. New York: Pantheon, 1981, 109 pp. (ages 14-adult).

      This is a collection of graphic drawings by survivors of
Hiroshima--a moving book, but not for the weak willed.

167.   Jarrell, Randall. "The Death of the Ball Turret Gunner,"
LITTLE FRIEND, LITTLE FRIEND, 1945; rpt. p. 547, EXPLORING
POETRY. M. L. Rosenthal and A. J. M. Smith, eds. New York:
Macmillan, 1967, 758 pp. (ages 12-adult).

      This concise poem (an adult poem often included in high
school English classes) juxtaposes the cold views of the
"State" with the human condition of "mother," linking birth
and death and offering a sharp view of the pathos of war.

168.   Jerome, Judson. "Deer Hunt." see Dunning, Stephen.

169.   Jones, Cordelia. NOBODY'S GARDEN. Illustrated by Victor
Ambrus. New York: Charles Scribner's Sons, 1966, 190 pp.
(10-adult).

     Bridget Sanders, twelve-years-old, was orphaned in World
War II and after the war moved in with her aunt and uncle in
London.
     She is quiet, numb from the war and tragedy of her
parents' death. On the other hand, Hilary, a classmate, is
not the least bit shy and decides to make Bridget an immediate
friend. As the book follows the ups and downs of their
developing friendship, it offers a good portrayal of postwar
London and the emotional struggle of a young girl overcoming
the loss of her parents.

170.   Jordan, June and Terri Bush, ed.   THE VOICE OF THE
CHILDREN. New York: Holt, Rinehart and Winston, 1970, 102 pp.
(ages 7-adult).

     This collection of poetry and prose is the result of a
Saturday morning writer's workshop lead by June Jordan and
Terri Bush in Brooklyn, New York, and contains several poems
dealing with violence and war, including "The Last Riot"
(about racial violence) and "Addition Problem" (about war in
general).
     The poems are sincere, sensitive, often bitter.

171.   Judson, Clara Ingram. GEORGE WASHINGTON: LEADER OF THE
     PEOPLE. Illustrated by Robert Frankenberg. Chicago:
     Wilcox and Follett, 1951, 224 pp. (ages 8-12).

     This is a dramatized biography of Washington that
attempts to correct some of the "mythical" pictures (both good
and bad) of previous biographers--but nevertheless tends to
over idealize him.
     It is a fast moving story. The black-and-white line
illustrations and impressionistic color illustrations are
average.

172.   Kay, Mara. IN FACE OF DANGER. Originally published as
STORMY WARNING, Great Britain, 1976. New York: Crown, 1977,
210 pp. (ages 10-adult).

     It is 1938. Ann Lindsay, having been taken by her
guardian, Uncle Dick, from her boarding school in England to
stay with him in Germany while he writes a series of articles,
is staying in the house of Frau Meixner, under the care of
Herr Doctor Fromm, after suffering a concussion in a car
accident that also put her uncle in the hospital. While she
is recovering, Ann thinks back over the visit to Germany. She
hadn't thought the rapidly advancing Nazi regime was bad--life
in Germany seemed prosperous. Her uncle knew better, and
predicted serious danger, not only for Germany, but for the
entire world.
     Uncle Dick had finished up his assigned articles and

decided the two of them should take a quick tour of Germany
before leaving (it might be their last chance, he had said).
That was when the accident had happened.

When Ann feels good enough to leave the bedroom, she does
so and meets Frau Meixner's son Peter, who wears the uniform
of Pimfe, the youngest division of Hitler's Youth Movement.
He immediately raises his right hand and says "Heil Hitler!"

As the story continues, Ann discovers that Frau Meixner
is hiding two Jewish girls in her attic. When Baron Von Ratth
is shot by a Jewish boy (at least that is the official story),
the Nazis have an excuse to step up persecution of the Jews,
and the story rises to a tense climax.

The "out-of-control" atmosphere, as the Nazis move toward
World War II, and some brave Christians attempt to save as
many of the Jews as possible, is clearly revealed, though
there is a bit too much melodrama about it.

173. Keith, Harold. RIFLES FOR WATIE. New York: Thomas Y.
Crowell, 1957, 332 pp. (ages 13-adult).

Jeff Bussey, a young Union soldier, is sent behind enemy
lines to find out where Stand Water, a Cherokee, is obtaining
rifles intended for the Union army. Jeff is captured and
pretends to be one of the Confederates, which puts him into a
position to understand their point of view.

The historic details (based on thorough research) are
vivid and accurate, the characterization works, and there is a
strong indictment of war, depicting its tragedy as well as its
heroism.

174. Kerr, Judith. WHEN HITLER STOLE PINK RABBIT.
Illustrated by the author. New York: Coward, McCann and
Geoghegan, 1972, 191 pp. (ages 8-12).

Anna, nine-years-old, and her family escape from Berlin
to Switzerland just before Nazis come into power. She chooses
between two stuffed animals--leaving her pink rabbit
behind--symbolizing leaving her life in Germany behind.

As the family moves from Switzerland to France to England
in search of a meager living, the story offers the solace of
the little everyday joys as more important than the large
transitions taking place.

There is little bitterness or self-pity, and the story is
about people who care about education and mutual respect.
However, the characters are somewhat stereotyped, and Anne
seems too mature for her age--though such experiences do
mature children rapidly. All in all, it is a good book,
overshadowed by a great number of even better books about the
subject.

175. Kerr, M. E. GENTLEHANDS. New York: Harper and Row, 1978,
183 pp. (ages 12-adult).

M. E. Kerr, author of several bluntly realistic and
controversial novels for children, including DINKY HOCKER
SHOOTS SMACK!, offers here the story of Buddy Boyle, a teenage
boy, whose mother has been estranged from her father (Grandpa
Trenker) for many years--though no one has ever told Buddy

why. One day Buddy decides to take Skye Pennington, a girl
friend, to visit Grandpa Trenker. As the story unfolds, Buddy
gets to know and care about his grandfather, who appears to be
a very cultured and kind man. Then, to Buddy's shock and
sadness, he finds out that his Grandpa Trenker (Gentlehands),
was once a Nazi concentration camp torturer and is still
involved with other Nazi war criminals!

The book raises questions about appearances and reality
and leaves the reader with an uneasy picture of a kind yet
cruel man.

176. Kjerdian, David. THE ROAD FROM HOME: THE STORY OF AN
ARMENIAN GIRL. New York: Greenwillow Press, 1979, pp. (ages
12-adult).

This story of survival is a fictionalized account of
David Kjerdian's mother, and deals with the persecution and
destruction of Armenian Christians by the Turkish Moslems.

177. Knight, Clayton. WE WERE THERE AT THE NORMANDY INVASION.
Historical Consultant Major General Ralph Royce, U.S.A.F. New
York: Grosset and Dunlap, 1956, 179 pp. (ages 12-adult).

Clayton Knight, a former airplane pilot in World War I
and Associated Press special correspondent in World War II,
both wrote and illustrated this fictional history of the
Normandy Invasion, one of a series of "We Were There" books
meant to provide objective, accurate accounts of important
moments in history.

The information it presents is detailed and correct and
the tone of it is standard 1950s, pleasant (it has a John
Wayne movie "feel" to it. The illustrations are black-
and-white line drawings meant to be realistic, thought, at
times, the proportions are slightly off and, though filled
with line, the detail is often sketchy.

The historical consultant for the book, Major General Ralph
Royce, Deputy Commander of the Ninth Air Force, was the senior
air officer afloat during the invasion of France.

178. Knox, Esther Melbourne. SWIFT FLIES THE FALCON: A STORY
OF THE FIRST CRUSADE. Illustrated by Ruth King. New York: John
C. Winston, 1939, 245 pp. (ages 12-adult).

Gareth and Margaret's father Roderick, the Earl of
Penbridge, has gone off to fight in the Holy Wars, leaving
Uncle Howell as their guardian. Uncle Howell, however, has
plans for ridding himself of them and seizing their father's
castle. Their only hope is to escape and head for Jerusalem.
Uther, an old Monk, and a friend of Roderick, decides to
journey with them, and they escape with a band of traveling
minstrels.

The book then follows their travels, which, truthfully,
are not all that exciting, until they reach the walls of the
Holy City, where they discover that their father has been
killed, and Gareth (Edgar) takes his place, becoming,
apparently, a man.

The "Bibliography" is a simple list of source materials
that were used to give the story its historically accurate

background.

179. Knox, Rose B. GRAY CAPS. Illustrated by Manning de V.
Lee. New York: Doubleday, Doran and Company, 1932, 304 pp.
(ages 12-16).

     This book offers a view of life in the South just before,
during, and just after the Civil War. It does not spend much
time debating whether that life style (including slavery) was
good or bad. Nevertheless, from the second scene, when Cary
and Bud fight over who should and who should not have the
right to beat on Cary's body servant (slave), referred to as a
"nigger," the reader is forced to confront the ethics of a
society based on slavery.
     The characters do not seem to grow or change through the
story, and in fact, their world has changed little by the end
of the story. After the war, the main family retains its
mansion, its money, and its slaves (though technically they
are now free). Apparently, the view expressed is that the
North may have won the war, but that very little has changed
as a result of it.
     Nevertheless, the characters are life-like, the sense of
scene is well detailed and realistic, and the events of the
Civil War do loom in the background (and in fact, time-and-
time again, break into the family's world).

180. Kohn, Bernice. ONE SAD DAY. Illustrated by Barbara Kohn
Isaac. New York: Third Press, Joseph Okpaku, 1971, 42 pp. (all
ages).

     The Spots are a peaceful, happy people who live in the
country. In another land, the stripes live peacefully in a
city environment. Everyone is content and happy. Then the
Stripes make war on the Spots, and everything and everyone on
earth is destroyed. This is an excellent, straight-forward
allegory of war, its senselessness, and the sad results, for
"war kills."

181. Kuskin, Karla. JERUSALEM: SHINING STILL. Illustrated by
David Frampton. New York: Harper and Row, 1987, 27 pp. (ages
5-8).

     This well illustrated book gives an overview of the
history of Jerusalem, 3000 years filled with conflict,
beginning with the battles of David, its founder and the
subsequent rule of his son Solomon, then covering the
seemingly endless stream of its conquorers--Nebuchadnezzar,
the Babylonians, the Greeks, the Romans (under Herald and
Hadrian and Constantine), the Persians, the Moslems, the
Egyptians, the Seljuks, the Crusaders, the Muslems (Saladin),
the Mameluke Egyptians, the Ottoman Turks, the British--all
bringing their own religious and way of life, leaving
Jerusalem as it is today. The British have gone. The Jews
and the Arabs fight a bitter war, and Jerusalem is torn and
battered.
     Yet Jerusalem, as presented in this book, still "shines."
The book offers a loving history of what is, perhaps, the most
emotionally charged city in the world--a city filled with

conflict.

182. Langton, Jane. THE FRAGILE FLAG. New York: Harper and
Row, 1984, 275 pp. (ages 9-12).

      Nine-year-old Georgie Hall (a very determined child)
leads a march of children from Massachusetts to Washington to
protest the President's new missile, which is capable of
destroying the earth.
      It's all a beautifully drawn realistic-fantasy, an
obvious plea for peace, an anti-missile, anti-war book.

183. Lawrence, Louise. CHILDREN OF DUST. New York: Harper and
Row, 1985, 183 pp. (ages 12-16).

      This is a graphic three part novel about the possible
long-term effects of a nuclear holocaust that projects
strangely mutilated children for successive generations.
      It has a fast pace to it, and the characters are decently
developed. However, the rapid evolutionary changes are hard
to believe and some of the plot is improbable.
      It is, all in all, an average novel, but one of few that
deal with long term effects of a possible nuclear war,
especially in terms of genetic mutations.

184. Lawson, Don, ed. GREAT AIR BATTLES; WORLD WARS I AND II.
New York: Lothrop, 1968, 223 pp. (ages 12-16).

      This is a collection of short, fast paced, accounts of
some of the air battles of the two World Wars by such people
as Winston Churchill and Quentin Reynolds. Don Lawson's
commentary is knowledgeable and affectionate. There are
several photographs of fighters and bombers.

185. Lawson, John. THE SPRING RIDER. New York: Crowell, 1968,
147 pp. (ages 11-13).

      Jacob and Gray (his sister) meet Sergeant Hannibal, a
young Union soldier who died many years ago in the Civil War,
but returns to the battlefield briefly each spring. Hannibal
falls in love with Gray, but realizes that the only way he can
keep her is for her to die and return with him. He must
choose between the eternal questions of war and peace, love
and sacrifice.
      The entire story has a sadness to it, and reveals how
precious life is.

186. Leaf, Munro. A WAR-TIME HANDBOOK FOR YOUNG AMERICANS.
New York: Frederick A. Stokes, 1942, 64 pp. (ages 3-7).

      This is a strong help-your-country-win-the-war guide for
children about how to act during World War II--very didactic.
It is more of interest as a curiosity of what some picture
book writers were doing to help the war effort than anything
else.

187.   Leaf, Munro. THE STORY OF FERDINAND. Illustrated by
Robert Lawson. Viking Press, 1936; New York: Puffin Books,
1977, 70 pp. (ages 3-7).

"Once upon a time in Spain" there was a bull who would
rather sit in the field and smell the flowers then fight.
That is the story of Ferdinand. Unfortunately, the day the
men come from Madrid to find ferocious bulls for the bull-
fights, Ferdinand gets stung by a bee, causing him to jump
around and snort, which makes the men think Ferdinand the most
ferocious bull in the field. But when Ferdinand is brought
into the ring to fight all he does is sit and smell the
flowers. "So they had to take Ferdinand home. And for all I
know he is sitting there still, under his favorite cork tree,
smelling the flowers just quietly. He is very happy."
The book can be read as a satire on the "sport" of bull
fighting (a bloody sport) and by extension as a stance against
violence and war in general.

188. Leichman, Seymour. THE BOY WHO COULD SING PICTURES.
Illustrated by the author. Garden City: New York: Doubleday,
1968, 59 pp. (ages 5-10).

Author/illustrator Seymour Leichman has offered a picture
book about a boy, Ben, who found he could sing pictures (when
he sang, pictures appeared). But the pictures came from the
people he sang for; he had no control over what they were; and
when he sang for the king and the court of warriors who all
loved war, the pictures were sad and showed the evil of the
king's manner of ruling. At first Ben was thrown in the
dungeon for showing how bad the king's rule was. However,
when the poor peasants of the kingdom begged for Ben's
release, the king realized the badness of his ways, and Ben
was released.
The happy ending happens too easily, has a false note to
it, but the ideas and the gentle humor are well presented. It
is similar to Uwe Friesel's TIM, THE PEACE MAKER in both
content and style.

189. Levertov, Denise. "The Alters in the Street," THE SORROW
DANCE. New Directions, 1966, 1 pp. (ages 14-adult).

This excellent poem depicts the Buddhist campaign of
passive non-resistance to the Vietnam war in 1966--Viet-
namese children building alters in the streets of Saigon and
Hue.
It offers a blunt picture of youth ("here a boy / with
red stumps for hands") suffering from the war that surrounds
them.
Denise Levertov is a highly respected contemporary poet
for adults.

190. Levitin, Sonia. JOURNEY TO AMERICA. Illustrated by
Charles Robinson. New York: Atheneum, 1971, 150 pp. (ages
8-12).

Lisa Platt tells us her story. It is February 7, 1938,
and her family has decided it must leave Berlin for America.

Germany is no longer safe for Jews. Her father makes his
secret escape first. Lisa, Anne and Ruth (her sisters), and
her mother follow, but not in secret. It is a difficult
journey for them. Since the Nazis only allow them to leave
with very few items, and almost no money, they are poor. Ruth
and Lisa must live in a cruel foster care home for a while.
Finally, they are reunited with their father in America.
    This is one of many good books dealing with the
Holocaust, most of them very similar. Taken together, they
offer an amazing documentation of human strength and dignity
in the face of the terrifying darkness. Some of the other
books include: ANNE FRANK: THE DIARY OF A YOUNG GIRL by Anne
Frank; YOUNG MOSHE'S DIARY: THE SPIRITUAL TORMENT OF A JEWISH
BOY IN NAZI EUROPE by Moshe Flinker, and NEVER TO FORGET: THE
JEWS OF THE HOLOCAUST by Milton Meltzer.

191.   Levoy, Myron. ALAN AND NAOMI. New York: Harper and Row,
1977, 192 pp. (ages 10-adult).

    Naomi, a young girl, has been badly traumatized by Nazi
cruely. She has now moved into New York with the Liebermans,
Alan's neighbors. Alan tries to make friends with her. But
her suffering has been too brutal.
    This is one of the best books written about the shock and
the aftermath of the Holocaust. The tragedy hits home.

192.   Lewis, C. S. THE CHRONICLES OF NARNIA: THE LION, THE
WITCH AND THE WARDROBE (A STORY FOR CHILDREN), 1950, 186 pp.;
PRINCE CASPIAN (THE RETURN TO NARNIA), 1951, 216 pp.; THE
VOYAGE OF THE "DAWN TREADER", 1952, 216 pp.; THE SILVER CHAIR,
1953, 217 pp.; THE HORSE AND HIS BOY, 1954, 217 pp.; THE
MAGICIAN'S NEPHEW, 1955, 186 pp.; THE LAST BATTLE, 1956, 184
pp. Pictures adapted from illustrations by Pauline Baynes. New
York: Collier Books, 1970. (ages 8-adult).

    C. S. Lewis, a highly respected British medievalist, well
known for his literary criticism, Christian apologetics and
such scholarship as the ALLEGORY OF LOVE, has achieved his
reputation in children's literature for the well known, yet
highly controversial CHRONICLES OF NARNIA.
    Before going any further, it should be emphasized that
the seven-volume saga is not a Christian allegory (though
there are allegorical elements in it), as C. S. Lewis states
in "Sometimes Fairy Stories May Say Best What's to be Said"
(OF OTHER WORLDS: ESSAYS AND STORIES. Edited by Walter Hooper.
Harcourt Brace Jovanovich, 1966):

> Some people seem to think that I began by asking
> myself how I could say something about Christi-
> anity to children; then fixed on fairy tale as an
> instrument; then collected information about
> child-psychology and decided what age group I'd
> write for; then drew up a list of basic Christian
> truths and hammered out 'allegories' to embody
> them. This is all pure moonshine. I couldn't
> write in that way at all. Everything began with
> images; a faun carrying an umbrella, a queen on
> a sledge, a magnificent lion. At first there wasn't
> even anything Christian about them; that ele-

ment pushed itself in of its own accord.   It was
part of the bubbling.

These Christian allegorical elements then get mixed in
with pure fantasy.   C. S. Lewis continues:

Then came the Form.   As these images sorted themselves into events (i.e., became a story) they
seemed to demand no love interest and no close
psychology.   But the Form which excludes these
things is the fairy tale.

The mixture of allegory and fairytale cannot but hurt the
saga, as pure fantasy must be separated from reality (even
literal or real world spirituality) in order to express itself
in the symbolic mode proper to fantasy and myth.   That is not
to say that fantasy cannot relate Christian values (which
most, perhaps all, do), but rather that each fantasy or myth
must be whole and of itself (just as the Christian myth could
never work if it were an allegory of some other myth).
If the reader can forget the obvious mixing in of
Christian one-on-one allegories, i.e., Aslan equals Christ,
and see them more as comparable elements, i.e., Aslan is
Christ-like, then it is possible to judge whether the saga
works or not.
And, though it has many flaws (some surprising from a
scholar of Lewis' ability, and a man who has spoken so in
opposition to those very flaws, "On Three Ways of Writing for
Children"), for example, the tendency to talk down to children
(i.e., such phrases as, "I hope you know what I mean by a
voice sounding pale," THE LION THE WITCH AND THE WARDROBE, p.
96), the poor dialogue (i.e., children speaking in ways it is
hard to believe children would speak, for example, saying "By
Jove" and "Great Scott" regularly), the narrow, strict views
of good and bad based on conformity and submission (i.e.,
Aslan is not to be questioned--only obeyed), and the poor
delineation of the children and their lack of growth and
change throughout the series, it is a good saga.
Lewis has created a "secondary world" (to use J. R. R.
Tolkien's terminology), which contains the wonder necessary
for fantasy.   It has the feel of myth and miracle--of Joy--,
and as does all High Fantasy, it is a presentation of the
battle of good evil on a worldwide scale.   And finally,
children respond strongly to it.   In fact, several of today's
greatest writers of children's literature, i.e., Katherine
Paterson, have claimed that the CHRONICLES OF NARNIA were
their favorite books as a child.
The final book of the series, THE LAST BATTLE received
the 1956 Carnegie Medal.
C. S. Lewis and J. R. R. Tolkien were, at least for a
time, close friends, and their views on fantasy (highly
respected today) emerged out of a mutual exchange of ideas.
Therefore, anyone wishing to come to terms with C. S. Lewis
should also study Tolkien, especially his "Tree and Leaf"
essay and his own famous high fantasy, THE HOBBIT and THE
TRILOGY OF THE RINGS.

193. Lifton, Betty Jean and Thomas C. Fox. CHILDREN OF
VIETNAM. Photographs by Thomas C. Fox. New York: Atheneum,
1972, 118 pp. (ages 12-adult).

Written just before the official end to an unofficial
war, this is an extremely moving testiment to the children of
Vietnam. Both Betty Jean Lifton and Thomas C. Fox spent time
in Vietnam, studying the children. "Studying" is too cold a
term; Thomas C. Fox states:

> It has been nearly five years now that I have
> lived and worked in Vietnam. During this time few
> moment have been as painful and fatiguing as
> those spent with the war's victimized children.

Earlier, he gave this example of what he had experienced:

> I cannot forget the day a forty-year-old
> peasant walked near his village the day after
> it was bombed by American jet planes. In his
> arms he held the limp, lifeless body of his
> four-year-old daughter. He looked into my eyes
> and said, "Tell President Johnson how my daughter
> died."

Near the beginning of the short, simple, powerful
introduction, Betty Lifton states:

> None of the children you will read about has
> ever known peace. The cycle of their lives is
> determined by troop movements and air raids,
> rather than the harvesting of crops. For them
> hunger, fear, and death are as regular as the
> seasons.
> They are the children of war.

CHILDREN OF VIETNAM is a powerful book, must reading for
anyone wanting a human perspective on war.

194. Lifton, Betty Jean. RETURN TO HIROSHIMA. Photographs by
Eikoh Hosoe. Mural Paintings by Mr. and Mrs. Iri Maraki. New
York: Athenuem, 1970, 91 pp. (ages 10-adult).

This excellent book presents both superb black-and-white
photographs and knowledgeable commentary on the bombing of
Hiroshima and its subsequent rebuilding. Those who might not
want children to be exposed to the destruction of atomic
weapons should be forewarned that some of the photographs
offer bluntly graphic evidence of the horror resulting from
the bomb in the form of mutilated bodies.
There are also four impressive mural paintings by Mr. and
Mrs. Iri Maruki depicting humans just after the bombing.
The commentary includes definitions of Japanese words
connected to the bombing (i.e., "The strength of the
"pikadon," the flash boom, as the bomb came to be called, was
equivalent to twenty thousand tons of TNT"), comparisons with
current atomic power (i.e., "We are making bombs with a
thousand times that strength today."), discussions of Peace
Park, Peace Museum, and the Atomic Dome ("It's wounded
presence shall continue to preside over the city."), the
Atomic Bomb Hospital ("Sometimes it is said that all roads in
Hiroshima lead to the Atomic Hospital."), several survivors of
the explosion ("'For the next seventeen years I was fine,' she

tells you, 'Then suddenly I started getting dizzy and needing
blood transfusions.'")
     However, the book does not dwell only on the tragedy of
the bombing. It also offers a picture of contemporary
Hiroshima (i.e.,"But the pride of the city is its baseball
stadium, which houses the Hiroshima Carps.").
     The book should be read in conjunction with John Hersey's
HIROSHIMA, Misuji Ibuse's BLACK RAIN and Toshi Maruki's
HIROSHIMA NO PIKA.

195. Lionni, Leo. SWIMMY. Illustrated by the author, New
York: Pantheon, 1963, 30 pp. (ages 3-5).

     Wonderful color illustrations highlight this tale of
Swimmy, a small black fish who bands together with a school of
other small fish to look like one big fish and scare away the
real giant fish who threaten them.

196. Little, Jean. HEY WORLD, HERE I AM. Illustrated by
Barbara Di Lella. Toronto: Kids Can Press, 1986, 64 pp. (ages
5-10).

     Jean Little attributes this collection of poetry to Kate
Bloomfield, a character (a young girl) in one of her earlier
books, LOOK THROUGH MY WINDOW.
     The prose poems are fresh, alive and capture well the
voice of a child. Some of them, such as "Wars" and "Maybe a
Fight," deal with conflict and resolution.

197. Lobel, Anita. POTATOES, POTATOES. Illustrated by the
author. New York: Harper and Row, 1967, 48 pp. (ages 4-10).

     With a sparse text and highly detailed pencil drawings
(and a few touches of color), Anita Lobel offers a parable of
war. A peasant woman's two sons are attracted to war and join
opposing armies (becoming a general and a commander respec-
tively). Later, they lead their starving armies back their
mother's farm, but she will not feed them until they stop the
war--which they do.
     The drawings are excellent, but the solution to the war
is too easily accomplished.

198. Longfellow, Henry Wadsworth. "Paul Revere's Ride," TALES
OF A WAYSIDE INN, 1863; rpt. pp. 184-187, THE GOLDEN TREASURE
OF POETRY. Edited by Louis Untermeyer. Illustrated by Joan
Walsh Anglund. New York: Golden Press, 1959, 324 pp. (all
ages).

     One of the better known poems of the American Revolution,
this is Longfellow's rendition of how Paul Revere spread the
alarm of British General Gage's planned capturing of Samuel
Adams and John Hancock, leading to the battle of Lexington.

199. Longfellow, Henry Wadsworth. "The Skeleton in Armor,"
BALLADS AND OTHER POEMS, 1841; rpt., pp. 173-175, THE GOLDEN

TREASURY OF POETRY. Illustrated by Joan Walsh Anglund. Edited
by Louis Untermeyer. New York: Golden Press, 1959, 324 pp.
(all ages).

Believing that an old skeleton dug up near Fall River,
Massachusetts, was that of a Viking warrior, Longfellow wrote
this poem, a tale of a norse warrior.
In a review of it, Edgar Allen Poe stated, "In 'The
Skeleton in Armor' we find a pure and perfect thesis
artistically treated. . . . The metre is simple, sonorous,
well-balanced, and fully adapted to the subject."

200. Lopshire, Robert. I AM BETTER THAN YOU. Illustrated by
the author. New York: Harper and Row, 1968, 64 pp. (ages 4-8).

Sam and Pete, two lizards, play the "I am better than
you" game, finally attempting to prove they can be more than
they are, realizing it, and agreeing to stop trying to better
each other.
The book is written in the easy to read language standard
for an "I Can Read" book, and both the illustrations and
writing are done in a light, humorous style.
It offers a simple lesson on cooperation versus
competition for younger readers.

201. Lord Byron (George Gordon). "The Destruction of
Sennacherib," 1815; rpt., p. 143, THE GOLDEN TREASURY OF
POETRY, ed., Louis Untermeyer. Illustrated by Joan Walsh
Anglund. New York: Golden Press, 1959, pp. 324. (all ages).

Lord Byron (1788-1824) was a fearless, daring, rebellious
man who died young while fighting for freedom in Greece. This
poem tells of the Assyrian king Sennacherib's siege of Jerusalem recorded in the Second Book of Kings, Old Testament.
The angel of Jehovah destroyed Assyrian's camp before he could
destroy Jerusalem.
The poem is a flamboyant recounting of this event.

202. Lunn, Janet. THE ROOT CELLAR. Endpaper Map by N. R.
Jackson. New York: Charles Scribner's Sons, 1983, 229 pp.
(ages 12-adult).

The characters and settings of this book are so well
drawn that, in spite of its obvious fantasy elements of ghosts
and time-travel, it seems a realistic novel. It explores,
among other things, the implications of displacement. The
main character, Rose, an orphan, who has spent her childhood
in the tightly controlled world of her grandmother, travelling
around the world, is sent to live with her Aunt Nan, who live
in an unkept house in the middle of nowhere with Uncle Bob,
and their four boys. Rose feels out of place and unwanted.
However, through another displacement, Rose learns what
it means to belong. This displacement is not one of space but
of time. Rose enters the property's root cellar and is
transported back in time, where she meets Will and Susan, who
become her first friends.
Though Will and Susan (as well as Aunt Nan and family)
are Canadians, Will decides to go off and fight in the
American Civil War (and readers are offered an interesting

Canadian perspective on that conflict). The tragedy of the
Civil War is brought subtly to life, neither sentimentalized
nor overly graphic.

Rose continues to travel back and forth through time,
while in the present, trying to become a member of Aunt Nan's
family, while in the past, trying to help Susan find Will, who
failed to return at the end of the war. While Rose goes
through various hardships, she grows and learns what it means
to give of oneself and to belong--a rite of passage from
childhood to adulthood.

Though not centering on the Civil War, the book offers a
seldom seen view of it from a Canadian perspective (Janet Lunn
is a naturalized Canadian citizen, having been born in the
United States).

Teenage girls should be especially attracted to it.

203. MacLeish, Archibald. "The Silent Slain." see Gregory,
Horace.

204. Magorian, Michelle. GOOD NIGHT, MR. TIM. New York:
Harper and Row, 1982, 318 pp. (ages 12-16).

Willie Beech, an abused boy, is evacuated from London
just prior to the outbreak of World War II. He learns from
Mr. Tim, the old man he stays with, to trust and not be
afraid.

It is a sentimental novel, not so much about war as about
the relationship of a boy and his evil mother and good
step-father.

205. Malkus, Alida Sims. WE WERE THERE AT THE BATTLE OF
GETTYSBURG. Illustrated by Leonard Vosburgh. Historical
Consultant Earl S. Miers. New York: Grosset and Dunlap, 1955,
176 pp. (ages 9-14).

In this standard "We Were There" book, Alida Sims Malkus
has included three dimensional characters (though they have a
"dated" quality in the same since that "Leave It to Beaver"
has a dated quality), and although there is the death and
destruction of war, there is an innocence not to be found in
good books written about war since the 1960s. The pictures in
black-and-white are also of a professional quality (realistic
portrayal of war) but have a "dated" feel about them. The
historical accuracy is defensible, though not as 'blunt' as
more contemporary graphic detail and honesty would demand.

All in all, if one is looking for a return to a simpler
time, a time before the Vietnam war and the various awakenings
of the 1960s, then this book will fit the bill.

206. Marks, Shirley. "Early Warning," OF QUARKS, QUASARS, AND
OTHER QUIRKS: QUIZZICAL POEMS FOR THE SUPERSONIC AGE.
Illustrated by Quentin Blake. Collected by Sara and John E.
Brewton and John Brewton Blackburn. New York: Crowell, 1977,
pp. (ages 10-adult).

Shirley Marks' parody on Paul Revere's ride suggests the
possibility of annihilation if a missile hits the United

States.

207.   Maruki, Toshi. HIROSHIMA NO PIKA. New York: Lothrop, Lee
& Shepard Books, 1982, 48 pp.; Japan: Komine Shoten, 1980.
(ages 10-adult).

      The book follows the experiences of Mii and her family
from the bombing of Hiroshima through the effects of the Atom
Bomb disease years later. Though it is a picture book, it is
filled with graphic illustrations and detailed discussions
aimed at an audience beyond the age of a young child, as the
following excerpt indicates:

              Mii never grew after that day. Many years have
              passed, and she is still the same size she was
              when she was seven years old. "It is because
              of the Flash from the bomb," her mother says.
              Sometimes Mii complains that her head itches,
              and her mother parts her hair, sees something
              shiny, and pulls it out of her scalp with a pair
              of tweezers. It's a sliver of glass, imbedded
              when the bomb went off years ago, that has worked
              its way to the surface.

      The book is a powerful anti-war statement. In the
epilogue, Toshi Maruki states:

              I am now past seventy years old. I have neither
              children nor grandchildren. But I have written
              this book for grandchildren everywhere. It took
              me a very long time to complete it. It is very
              difficult to tell young people about something
              very bad that happened, in the hope that their
              knowing will help keep it from happening again.

      Obviously, Toshi Maruki meant the book for children.
However, as with several other recent picture books, the
detailed, dark subject matter makes it hard to decide just who
the audience should be.

208.   Mazer, Harry. THE LAST MISSION. New York: Delacorte
Press, 1979, 182 pp. (ages 10-adult).

      A member of the 398th Bomb Group of the Eighth Air Force
during World War II, Harry Mazer offers here the story of Jack
Raab, a fifteen-year-old Jewish boy, who tells his family he
is traveling west in 1944, but instead falsifies his age and
joins the United States Air Corps and subsequently is captured
by the Germans.
      The books is a well written account (graphic at time--but
less so than many) of World War II from a somewhat unusual
angle. It is a boy's adventure story.

209.   McGowen, Tom. GEORGE WASHINGTON. Richard B. Morris,
Consulting Editor. New York: Franklin Watts, 1986, 64 pp.
(ages 8-12).

      This is a brief, straight-forward biography of George

Washington from his youth in Virginia to his death. It has
several black-and-white photographs, an index, and a brief
bibliography.

210. McNeer, May. AMERICA'S ABRAHAM LINCOLN. Illustrated by
Lynd Ward. Boston: Houghton Mufflin, 1957, 119 pp. (ages
10-12).

     This version of Abe Lincoln's biography has more of a
fictional, storytelling quality about it than most. The
illustrations (some in color) have a nice atmospheric feel
about them.
     Readers should find the style appealing.

211. Meader, Stephen W. THE MUDDY ROAD TO GLORY. Illustrated
by George Hughes. New York: Harcourt, Brace & World, 1963, 190
pp. (ages 12-15).

     Prolific writer of popular adventure stories for
teenagers, Stephen W. Meader presents here the story of
sixteen-year-old Ben Everett, who joins the Twentieth Maine
regiment of the Army of the Potomac to fight in the Civil War.
He experiences the hardships of war, fighting in several
smaller battles, until he is captured and sent to the prison
camp on Belle Isle. He eventually escapes and fights again
with his regiment until Lee's surrender at Appomattox.

212. Meltzer, Milton. AIN'T GONNA STUDY WAR NO MORE: THE
STORY OF AMERICA'S PEACE SEEKERS. New York: Harper and Row,
1985, 268 pp. (ages 10-16).

     This is one of several excellent books by Milton Meltzer
aimed at secondary school students (including THE TERRORISTS,
THE HUMAN RIGHTS BOOK, and NEVER TO FORGET: THE JEWS OF THE
HOLOCAUST) that offer an alternative to the standard pro-war
or war-is-inevitable history books generally in use,
presenting a history that seldom gets into assigned history
books, and should be read in conjunction with them.
     Meltzer has thoroughly researched the history of American
pacifists and pacifist movements and presents an honest,
straight forward portrayal of those people and movements, from
the early Christians, to the Quakers, lead by George Fox, to
Representative Jeanett Rankin of Montana (though the caption
under her photograph incorrectly says she is from Minnesota),
the only congressman to vote against entrance into both World
Wars, to the Vietnam draft resisters and current United
States/Soviet Union arms build-up. It will make those who
read it, whether hawks or doves, stop and think about war and
dissent, freedom and truth, and individual responsibility and
choice.

213. Meltzer, Milton. BOUND FOR THE RIO GRANDE: THE MEXICAN
STRUGGLE, 1845-1850. New York: Knopf, 1974, 279 pp. (ages
12-18).

     Meltzer offers another of his excellent histories, well
researched (though Seymour V. Commor in a review of the book

for THE WESTERN HISTORICAL QUARTERLY, Vol. 6, No. 4, Oct.,
1975, pp. 461-462, points out some flaws), of important events
in American history. Several original documents with
commentary are included, as is a chronology of important
dates.
    As usual, Meltzer does not gloss over the negative sides
of the United States involvement (i.e., the savage treatment
of the Indians).

214. Meltzer, Milton. GEORGE WASHINGTON AND THE BIRTH OF OUR
NATION. New York: Watts, 1986, 188 pp. (ages 10-18).

    Building on thorough research, Meltzer offers a straight
forward biography placed within the context of the times,
revealing the reasons for Washington's aristocratic views, his
reluctant role as commander of the American troops, and both
his flaws and successes as he learned and became competent in
his position,
    A good selection of black-and-white reproductions of
paintings, engravings, and the like, some maps, an index, and
a discussion of books for further reading--all add to the
value.

215. Meltzer, Milton. HUNTED LIKE A WOLF: THE STORY OF THE
SEMINOLE WAR. New York: Farrar, Straus and Giroux, 1972, 216
pp. (ages 10-18).

    This study of the Seminole War, written with Meltzer's
standard thorough research and documentation, including
photographs and a bibliography, presents the story of the
Seminoles' subjugation because of the greed, trickery, and
superior strength of a government bent on annexation of
Florida, because, as Henry Clay stated, "It fills a space in
our imagination."
    It is a well done account of a seldom considered part of
America's history.

216. Meltzer, Milton. NEVER TO FORGET: THE JEWS OF THE
HOLOCAUST. Harper and Row: New York, 1076, 217 pp. (ages
12-adult).

    Meltzer decided to write this book after reading a
pamphlet stating that American high school textbooks ignored
or only very briefly treated the subject of the Holocaust.
The book is divided into three pares: 1) anti-Semitism, its
history; 2) World War II and Hitler's use of it to destroy the
Jews; and 3) the Jewish resistance to their fate.
    As is usual, Meltzer based the book on thorough scholar-
ship of original sources (diaries, letters, eyewitness accounts, trials, songs, poems), many of them from the children.
    Without censoring it or making it melodramatic, Meltzer
presents a clear picture of the mass murder of six million
Jews (something high school students deserve to be exposed
to), for it is, as Meltzer points out, neither a mere
aberration nor the responsibility of only a small group of
people. Rather the entire world must take responsibility for
allowing it to take place.

217.   Meltzer, Milton. THE TERRORISTS. New York: Harper and Row, 1983, 216 pp. (ages 12-18).

Once again, Melvin Meltzer has provided a thoroughly researched, human view of a dark side of humanity. The book begins with a history of terrorism and ends with a consideration of the justification for terrorism (i.e., do the ends justify the means?).
In between, numerous specific incidents are dealt with--always with an attempt to understand the terrorists, their reasons, etc. The presentation is straight forward and easy to follow, and each terrorist group dealt with is placed in historical and political context. A biography is included.

218.   Meltzer, Milton. UNDERGROUND MAN. New York: Bradbury Press, 1972, 220 pp. (ages 12-18).

Milton Meltzer bases this fictionalized account of Joshua Bowen's activities for the Underground Railroad on the true fragmentary memoirs of a Northern farmboy, once again creating a thoroughly documented, historically accurate view of an important time in America's history. The black characters might have received a fuller, deeper characterization, but this is a minor oversight in what is a dramatic, thoughtful novel.

219.   Melville, Herman. "The Returned Volunteer," THE CRYSTAL CABINET: AN INVITATION TO POETRY. Edited by Horace Gregory and Myra Zaturenska. Wood Engravings by Diana Bloomfield. New York: Holt, Rinehart and Winston, 1962. (ages 12-adult).

This is a excellent example of Melville's war poetry.

220.   Merrill, Jean F. THE PUSHCART WAR. Illustrated by Ronni Solbert. New York: William R. Scott, 1964, 222 pp. (ages 9-12).

This is an excellent allegory of how wars begin, are escalated and are ultimately resolved. Author Jean F. Merrill states in her introduction:

> I have always believed that we cannot have
> peace in the world until "all of us" under-
> stand how wars start. And so I have tried to
> set down the main events of the Pushcart War
> in such a way that readers of all ages may
> profit from whatever lessons it offers.

In lively and detailed manner, Merrill relates the war, as if it were a real history of a real war between the trucks and the pushcarts of New York City. A great deal of humor is infused into a presentation of the cause, strategies and battles.
It all began with the daffodil massacre:

> The Pushcart War started on the afternoon of
> March 15, 1976, when a truck ran down a pushcart
> belonging to a flower peddler. Daffodils were
> scattered all over the street. The pushcart was

flattened, and the owner of the pushcart was
pitched headfirst into a pickle barrel.

221. Metzger, Larry. ABRAHAM LINCOLN. New York: Watts, 1987,
93 pp. (ages 9-12).

     This is a good, brief overview, written in a friendly
style (i.e., it begins "What an odd child Abraham Lincoln
was!"), and it presents the basic facts and ideas concerning
Lincoln in a clear manner. The black-and-white photographs
are well selected.
     It is for a slightly younger audience than Russell
Freedman's LINCOLN: A PHOTOBIOGRAPHY.

222. Miers, Earl Schenck. ABRAHAM LINCOLN. Consultant Paul M.
Angle. New York: American Heritage Publications, 1964, 153 pp.
(ages 10-15).

     This is a standard "American Heritage Junior Library"
non-fictional account of a great personage, in this case
Abraham Lincoln, filled with illustrations--kphotographs,
drawings, paintings, etc., and it gives a good, brief
overview.

223. Miklowitz, Gloria. AFTER THE BOMB. New York: Scholastic,
1985, 156 pp. (ages 10-15).

     Sixteen-year-old Philip Singer is a "typical" teenager
(he has a crush on his brother Matt's girlfriend, feels
awkward and inadequate, and has little concern about world
affairs--thinking he cannot influence them anyway). Then, a
one-megaton bomb explodes over his city while his father is
away. His mother is badly injured, his brother becomes sick
and weak, and Matt's girlfriend Carla is terrified. Philip
has to take charge.
     The book is a decent account of what might happen im-
mediately after a nuclear explosion. As it states in the
introductory "Note," the factual assumptions about the degree
of damage and likely assistance were drawn from research in
several books and extensive interviews.
     The characters are similar to Judy Blume's characters (a
bit flat predictable), and the plot is more a framework for
"teaching" about what it would be like after a nuclear
explosion than anything else. Nevertheless, it is a good book
for introducing youth in their early teens to the potential
seriousness of nuclear war.
     Gloria Miklowitz has written several other books for
teenagers, including THE WAR BETWEEN THE CLASSES, a book about
prejudice.

224. Minarik, Else Holmelund. NO FIGHTING, NO BITING.
Illustrated by Maurice Sendak. New York: Harper and Row, 1958;
rpt., 1978, 62 pp. (ages 4-6).

     Two children fight, mainly verbally, while their cousin
Joan reads a story about two little alligators who also fight
or quarrel with one another. Sendak's illustrations, with

their excellent facial expressions, offer a humorous extension
to the story.

225. Monjo, Ferdinand N. A NAMESAKE FOR NATHAN: BEING AN
ACCOUNT OF CAPTAIN NATHAN HALE BY HIS TWELVE-YEAR-OLD SISTER,
JOANNA. Illustrated by Eros Keith. New York: Coward, McCann
and Geoghegan, 1977, 127 pp. (ages 10-16).

        This fictionalized biography of Nathan Hale is based on
thorough research, which, as the author indicates in an
afterword "About this Story," reveals a mass of contra-
dictions, especially about Nathan Hale's final days. As the
author states, "We aren't ever going to know, for a certainty,
whether or not he ever said 'I only regret that I have but one
life to lose for my country.'"
        However, as the author also states, "We can be sure (from
what do know) that he lived and died in perfect consonance
with that lofty sentiment, whether he happened to speak those
words or not."
        The story is told from the perspective of Joanna Hale,
Nathan's sister, who was twelve at the time, and recounts the
events of 1776 as she and her family followed the activities
of her "attractive, forceful, and loveable" twenty-one-year-
old brother.

226. Monjo, Ferdinand N. THE DRINKING GOURD. Illustrated by
Fred Brenner. New York: Harper and Row, 1970, 62 pp. (ages
4-7).

        This "I Can Read History" book, developed from "The
Drinking Gourd," a song often sung by escaping slaves, is a
fictional account of a young boy, Tommie, who helps some
slaves escape into Canada.
        It presents a good, simple view of the issues and morals
of slavery.

227. Monjo, Ferdinand N. GETTYSBURG: TAD LINCOLN'S STORY.
Illustrated by Douglas Gorsline. New York: Dutton, 1976, 48
pp. (ages 6-10).

        This is a fictionalized story of the events and
circumstances surrounding the Battle of Gettysburg and the
dedication of the National Cemetary there in 1863 told through
the eyes of Tad Lincoln, Abraham Lincoln's favorite son, and
includes the famous Gettysburg address, which, in itself,
makes the book worthwhile. It goes:

                Fourscore and seven years ago our fathers
        brought forth on this continent a new nation,
        conceived in liberty and dedicated to the pro-
        position that all men are created equal. Now
        we are engaged in a great civil war, testing
        whether that nation, or any nation so conceived
        and so dedicated, can long endure. We are met
        on a great battlefield of that war. We have
        come to dedicate a portion of that field as a
        final resting place for those who here gave their

lives that that nation might live. It is al-
together fitting and proper that we should do
this. But, in a larger sense, we cannot dedi-
cate--we cannot consecrate--we cannot hallow--
this ground. The brave men, living and dead,
who struggled here have consecrated it far a-
bove our poor power to add or detract. The
world will little note nor long remember what
we say here, but it can never forget what they
did here. It is for us, the living, rather to
be dedicated here to the unfinished work which
they who fought here have thus far so nobly ad-
vanced. It is rather for us to be here dedicated
to the great task remaining before us--that from
these honored dead we take increased devotion to
that cause for which they gave the last full mea-
sure of devotion; that we here highly resolve that
these dead shall not have died in vain; that this
nation, under God, shall have a new birth of freedom; and that government of the people, by the
people, and for the people, shall not perish from
the earth.

The book does not detail the horrors of war and is, in
general, told in the voice of a boy speaking to children,
containing, perhaps, a too simplistic view of war and freedom
and life in general. The final passage goes:

Well, Pa believes that "his" country belongs to
"all" of us--not just to the ones of us who's
white. And when all those boys died at Gettysburg, that's what they was dying for--so's "all"
men could be free and equal, like we claim they
created.
At least that's what I take Pa to mean. Why
else would he say "a 'new' birth of freedom?"

It's hard to argue with such statements about equality
and freedom.

228. Monjo, Ferdinand N. PIRATES IN PANAMA. Illustrated by
Wallace Tripp. New York: Simon and Schuster, 1970, 64 pp.
(ages 6-9).

This is the story of Henry Morgan's capture of Panama in
1671, told in Monjo's style of short sentences arranged in
blank verse. As in his other books, the characters are overly
simplified and their acts, which in many cases are question-
able, are put in the best possible light.
In the "Afterword" Monjo indicates that Henry Morgan's
reputation is, after all, not so positive as some and the
story here presented would have us believe.
However, Monjo claims his version is close to that
currently told in Panama, which, assuming he is telling us the
truth, makes the book an introduction for adults interested in
the history and culture of Panama.
Henry Morgan and his pirates and their battles are
presented in much the same fun-filled, boyish exuberance as
those of Howard Pyle, though the telling is aimed at a younger
audience and not nearly as well done.

229. Monjo, Ferdinand N. THE VICKSBURG VETERAN. Illustrated
by Douglas Gorsline. New York: Simon and Schuster, 1971, 62
pp. (ages 6-10).

     This book is very similar in style to GETTYSBURG: TAD
LINCOLN'S STORY, also by Monjo. It is told from the eyes of
Frederick Dent Grant, General Ulysses S. Grant's oldest son,
twelve at the time of the capture of Vicksburg, and is an
account of that event, told in very short, simple statements
(though the captions under the illustrations are, at times,
more complex, apparently aimed at the adults who might be
reading the story to their children.
     It is a simple view of the battle, the Civil War, Ulysses
S. Grant, slavery in the South, and war in general. Children
should be exposed other views as well.
     The illustrations, black-and-white, realistic, thought
somewhat crude, in muted shades at times, in general, are more
realistic and carry more detailed descriptions of the
actuality of the war.

230. Monjo, Ferdinand N. ZENAS AND THE SHAVING MILL.
Illustrated by Richard Cutfari. New York: Coward, McCann and
Geoghegan, 1976, 48 pp. (ages 6-10).

     This fictionalized account of a young Quaker boy's
attempts to elude the ships of both the British and the
American rebels while sailing into Nantucket with needed
supplies for the Quakers, who have a tradition of non-violence
and, thus, are non-allied during the Revolutionary War, is
written in short sentences (almost a blank verse style--
similar to that used by Monjo in THE VICKSBURG VETERAN), an
obvious attempt to keep it readable for a younger audience,
and perhaps successful, though it has a sense of "talking down
to children" and falls short of the approaches of the like of
Dr. Seuss and Shel Silverstein.
     The illustrations are line drawings with a rough realism
to them--some shading and cross-hatching is used.
     Even with the somewhat overly simple views expressed, the
book has value, introducing children to several phrases of the
time (i.e., "Stopped by an American privateer (or "shaving
mill," as we sometimes call them"), presenting an often
overlooked aspect of the war, those who did not take sides,
and revealing, though only superficially, the Quaker religion.

231. Monsell, Helen A. BOY OF OLD VIRGINIA: ROBERT E. LEE.
Illustrated by Coltilde Embree Funk. New York: Bobbs-Merrill,
1937, 165 pp. (ages 6-10).

     This book about the childhood of Robert E. Lee (the final
two pages rapidly relate his adult accomplishments) is written
in simple prose (short, straight forward sentences and limited
vocabulary) and would make good reading for elementary school
students.
     It presents Robert E. Lee as a very likeable child and
takes the liberties of fiction to offer a possible view of
life at that time--a time when Robert's father was involved in
the Revolutionary War. However, the book is a bit too sweet
and pleasant at times.
     The illustrations by Funk, in the silhouette style of A.

Rackham, are excellent.

232. Moskin, Marietta D. I AM ROSEMARIE. New York: John Day,
1972, 190 pp. (ages 10-adult).

     This book is an excellent fictionalized biography of a
Jewish girl from the Netherlands who manages to live through
the horrors that her family encounters following the Nazi
occupation in 1940, covering the years from 1940-1945.
     The telling details of trying to have as normal a life as
possible under the horrible conditions of the concentration
camps make the story a better than average one, though there
are many excellent stories about this terrible part of human
history.
     In the "Author's Note" at the end of the novel, Marietta
D. Moskin dedicates the book to "all those who did not live to
tell about their sufferings," because "they should not be
forgotten."

233. Murray, Michele. THE CRYSTAL NIGHTS. New York: Seabury
Press, 1973, 310 pp. (ages 11-adult).

     It is 1938. Elly, age fifteen, and her immediate family
have moved out of Germany, but Jewish relatives remain behind.
The Holocaust is occurring, though distanced. For those who
have encountered (even if only through literature) the horrible actions of the concentration camps, the suffering of the
Jews, even those who are safely out of reach of the Nazis,
makes many of the family's actions understandable. However,
the characters are not likeable.
     This is a strange story, and it leaves its readers
struggling with the desire to feel sympathy for people who are
not easy to care about.

234. Navon, Yitzhuk. THE SIX DAYS AND THE SEVEN GATES.
Illustrated with Photographs (anon). Translated by Misha
Louvish. New York: Herzl Press, 1979, 22 pp. (ages 10-adult).

     This is a poetic version of the legend of the recapturing
of Jerusalem by the Israeli army. Each of the seven gates of
the city in turn steps forward and asks to be the gate by
which the city will be recaptured. The Lion's Gate, the gate
concerned with the lives of the people, is the one chosen.
     Large (often two full pages) black-and-white photographs
of contemporary Jerusalem and its gates accompany the text.
     The book is, of course, a religious call to war, though
the gate chosen is chosen because it wishes no more death.

235. Naylor, Phyllis Reynolds. THE DARK OF THE TUNNEL. New
York: Atheneum, 1985, 207 pp. (ages 12-adult).

     Eighteen-year-old Craig Sheldon finds out his mother has
terminal cancer. He, his eleven-year-old brother Lonnie, Big
Jim (brother of his dead father), and his mother all come into
strong focus as they struggle to deal with her immanent death.
     This personal tragedy is set against a fully realized
background of threatened nuclear war with Russia and the

community's attempts to prepare for it.

236. Neimark, Anne E. ONE MAN'S VALOR: LEO BAECK AND THE
HOLOCAUST. New York: Lodestar, 1986, 113 pp. (ages 13-adult).

    This is the biography of a man of exceptional fortitude
who stood up to Hitler and toiled endlessly to help his fellow
Jews endure the Nazi reign.
    It is a work of non-fiction that offers the human values
often found only in fiction, and is an inspiring read.

237. Nhuong, Huynh Quang. THE LAND I LOST: ADVENTURES OF A
BOY IN VIETNAM. Illustrated by Vo-Dinh Mai. New York: Harper
and Row, 1982, 115 pp. (ages 8-12).

    Huynh Quang Nhuong was born in Mytho, Vietnam, graduated
from Saigon University, and was drafted into the South Vietnamese army. While in battle, he was permanently paralyzed by
a gunshot wound, and moved to the United States in 1969 for
additional medical treatment.
    This book tells what life was like in Vietnam before the
war, ending when Ho Chi Minh's forces confronted the French
forces in Nhuong's hamlet, resulting in the killing of Tank,
Nhuong's dog. It is a worthwhile description of life in
Vietnam directly before the war.

238. Nicolay, Helen. THE BOY'S LIFE OF ABRAHAM LINCOLN.
Illustrated by Jay Hambidge, et al. New York: The Century
Company, 1917, 307 pp. (ages 12-18).

    While Helen Nicolay gets overly dramatic and a bit too
"gushy," this is a decent factual account of Lincoln's life
for older children.

239. O'Dell, Scott. SARAH BISHOP. Boston: Houghton Mifflin,
1980, 184 pp. (ages 12-adult).

    After the tragic deaths of her father and brother, who
took opposite sides in the Revolutionary War, Sarah rejects
civilization and heads for the wilderness, where she learns to
survive in a cave. However, after she goes through a series
of adventures, including being accused of witchcraft, it
becomes clear she will, in fact, move back into civilization,
in spite of her disillusionment with it.
    Along with messages about the stupidity of war and
superstition, this is a story of self-reliance and the courage
of the human spirit (common themes in Scott O'Dell's books).
Sarah Bishop is a compelling heroine, and the period and place
are well drawn. Teenage girls with be attracted to the story.

240. Ofek, Uriel. SMOKE OVER GOLAM: A NOVEL OF THE 1973 YOM
KIPPER WAR IN ISRAEL. Illustrated by Lloyd Bloom. Translated
by Israel I. Taslitt. New York: Harper and Row, 1979, 184 pp.
(ages 8-12).

    Uriel Ofek is one of Israel's most important writers of

children's fiction (having published over thirty-five books).
This book, written in the form of the memoirs of a
ten-year-old Israeli boy, tells of his friendship with Saleem,
a Syrian boy, and how it survives the war.
        It is a good book. The narrator is a real, likeable boy,
and the themes include peace and the importance of human
relationships.

241.   Oneal, Zibby. WAR WORK. Illustrated by George Porter.
New York: Viking Press, 1971, 251 pp. (ages 10-adult).

        This is an enjoyable novel about what it was like to be a
child in America during World War II, a time when, as Zibby
Oneal states, "It was as though the whole civilian population
in America had gone a little mad. Life was zany. As children, we were thrilled by the excitement of it all. We saw no
moral issue."
        Zoe, Rosie, and Joe decide to become spies (its their
"war work"). At first, it's just a game. Later, the game
turns serious.
        The characters are well rounded, real, and if Oneal's
statement is a true one (as it seems to be), the story
presents a side of the war seldom seen--that very innocent
view of the children not in the middle of the death and
destruction.

242.   Orgel, Doris. A CERTAIN MAGIC. New York: Dial Press,
1976, 176 pp. (ages 8-12).

        Though not as exciting or fast moving as another book by
Doris Orgel, THE DEVIL IN VIENNA, this book once again brings
readers into the terror of Nazi Germany. In this case,
eleven-year-old Jenny discovers her Aunt Trudl's copybook and
reads herself back into the child-evacuation from Nazi Germany
to England.
        Good and evil are handled in simple enough terms for
children to understand. The characters are believible and
sympathetic. And though a bit sentimental, the story is
likely to bring tears. It is a worthwhile read.

243.   Orgel, Doris. THE DEVIL IN VIENNA. New York: Dial Press,
1978, 246 pp. (ages 12-adult).

        Basing the characters and events on her own experiences
during the Nazi regime, Doris Orgel offers a compelling story
of the friendship of Inge, a Jewish girl, and Lieselotte, the
daughter of a violent Nazi.
        This is one of many excellent books on the Holocaust,
including MY ENEMY, MY BROTHER by James Forman, ANNE FRANK:
THE DIARY OF A YOUNG GIRL by Anne Frank, and I AM ROSEMARIE by
Marietta Moskin. In this case, the main character and her
family must submit to baptism in order to survive by escaping
to Yugoslavia.

244.   Orlev, Uri. THE ISLAND ON BIRD STREET. Translated by
Hillel Halkin. Boston: Houghton Mifflin, 1984, 162 pp. (ages
12-adult).

Uri Orlev spent 1939-41 hiding in a Warsaw ghetto with
his mother, who was eventually killed by the Nazis, and
younger brother. His father had already been captured by the
Russians.

This experience obviously influenced THE ISLAND ON BIRD
STREET, the 1981 Mordechai Bernstein Award winning story about
Alex, an eleven-year-old boy, whose father has been taken by
the German army for places unknown and mother has also dis-
appeared. Alex hides out in the upper floor of an abandoned
building on Bird Street, lowering a rope ladder to seek food
and fuel.

Life is brutal, and the boy has only his belief that his
father will return to keep him going. It is a story filled
with blunt confrontations of what life was like for a young
Jewish boy hiding in the Warsaw ghetto, including the "neces-
sity" to kill. But through all the darkness there are the
themes of hope, kindness, sharing, helping one another, and
even love. It is a good, realistic depiction of a horrible
event.

245. Patchen, Kenneth. FIRST WILL AND TESTAMENT. New York:
Padell, 1948, 177 pp. (ages 14-adult).

This collection of poetry and a few short pieces of drama
is filled with passionate outpourings of the human spirit,
many of them concerning war.
The final entry, "The Haunted City," ends:

> Humanity is a good thing. Perhaps we can
>   arrange the murder
> of a sizeable number of people to survive it.

The collection is aimed at older children who can
understand satire.

246. Pease, Howard. HEART OF DANGER. New York: Doubleday,
1946, 336 pp. (ages 12-16).

This World War II story follows Tod Moran, a third mate
on the American freighter Araby, and Rudy Behrens, a fireman
and ex-music-student, on a mission through Nazi territory,
Rudi's experiences at Buchenwald, and later, his looking back
on the war.
The book has a great deal of texture, provided by flash-
backs into Rudy's past, references to Beethoven's music, and
detailed settings, but it is unfocused and overly melodramatic.
The title comes from a comment by a Resistance worker:
"To conquer danger, one must go directly to its heart."

247. Phillips, Loretta and Prentice Phillips. TWO SILLY
KINGS. Illustrated by Warren Hunter. Austin, Texas: Steck,
1964, 32 pp. (ages 3-5).

This is a simple story about two kings who have a silly
quarrel, declare war, forget why they declared war, decide to
fight anyway (because of pride), are interrupted just before
the fighting begins by a boy playing a flute, end up dancing

and cheering, and decide not to fight.
        It is simplistic and does not offer an honest solution.
The illustrations in ink and watercolor are too busy to be
effective.

248.   Pratt, N. S. THE FRENCH REVOLUTION. Illustrated by
Elizabeth Hammond. New York: John Day, 1970, 128 pp. (ages
12-adult).

        This is part of "The Young Historian Books," a series
edited by Patrick Rooke intended as "a library of world history from ancient times to the present day." It contains a
table of main dates, a book list, and an index. The subject
matter of each section is indicated in the margin next to it.
There are also many illustrations, photographs and line drawings in various styles. The new drawings are done by Elizabeth Hammond. All add greatly to the text and help bring the
time period to life.
        The book offers an exciting narrative of the events
leading up to, including, and following the French Revolution,
and includes an analysis of why the revolution came about and
its significance for modern Europe. The theme of the book is
that revolutions (beginning with the French Revolution), with
all of their violence, are nevertheless what brought Europe
from a world of aristocratic privilege and despotism to a
world where men struggled for liberty and equality.
        It is a clearly organized, straight forward presen-
tation--a good introduction and overview to the subject.

249.   Pringle, Lawrence. NUCLEAR POWER: FROM PHYSICS TO
POLITICS. New York: Macmillan, 1979. (ages 12-adult).

        Pringle traces the development of nuclear power to 1970,
discussing both the facts and controversy.

250.   Pringle, Lawrence. NUCLEAR WAR: FROM HIROSHIMA TO
NUCLEAR WINTER. Hillside, New Jersey: Enslow Publ., 1985, 128
pp. (ages 12-18).

        This is a thorough, factual presentation of the scien-
tific and military aspects of nuclear war. It offers a history (beginning with Hiroshima) and projects the results of a
future nuclear holocaust.
        There are many illustrations (black-and-white photo-
graphs, maps, diagrams), a glossary, a bibliography, and an
index.
        The language is aimed at a teenage audience, and the book
is filled with blunt facts that should raise questions for a
discussion on the subject.
        Lawrence Pringle (who also writes under Sean Edmund) is a
past editor of NATURE AND SCIENCE and has written many books
for youth on biology and the environment.

251.   Provensen, Alice and Martin Provensen. A PEACEABLE
KINGDOM: THE SHAKER ABECEDARIUS. Afterword by Richard Meran
Barsam. Illustrated by the authors. New York: Viking, 1978,
48 pp. (ages 3-6).

This is the Shaker alphabet, well illustrated with details of Quaker life and containing inscriptions expressing Quaker beliefs. Taken from the "Shaker Manifesto" of 1882, it is filled with pleas for peace.

A feel for the rhythmic flow of it can be gained from the first verses:

Alligator, Beetle, Porcupine, Whale
Bobolink, Panther, Dragonfly, Snail

As the poem proceeds through a listing of the animals, the pen-and-ink and watercolor illustrations intersperse Shaker people, objects and motifs with the animals.

252. Reck, Franklin, M. BEYOND THE CALL OF DUTY. New York: Thomas Y. Crowell, 1945, 168 pp. (ages 10-16).

Franklin M. Reck tells the stories of the first sixteen winners of the Medal of Honor in the Army Ground Forces, plus two Army Air Force officers, during World War II. It is written in a highly reverent manner, supporting the country's citation statement about winners of this award:

For conspicuous gallantry and intrepidity involving risk of life above and beyond the call of duty in action with the enemy.

253. Reiss, Johanna. THE UPSTAIRS ROOM. New York: Crowell, 1972. (ages 9-14).

This autobiographical story of the Jewish holocaust tells of Annie and her older sister, who are hidden in the upstairs room of their Dutch farm home for what they expect will be only a few weeks. However, the weeks stretch into over two years.   The courage of both the Jews and the non-Jews who helped them is revealed.

254. Remarque, Erich Maria. ALL QUIET ON THE WESTERN FRONT. Boston: Little, Brown, 1929, 291 pp. (ages 12-adult.

This simple, direct, concise indictment of war is told from the viewpoint of nineteen-year-old Paul, who serves with two of his classmates as a common German soldier in the trenches of World War I. By the end of the novel, though he is still alive, he is spiritually dead.

255. Reynolds, Quenton. THE BATTLE OF BRITAIN. Illustrated by Clayton Knight. New York: Random House, 1953, 182 pp. (ages 8-12).

This simplistic story of the Battle of Britain, which began on August 8, 1940 and ended on October 31, 1940, has a condescending tone.

256. Richards, Allan. "A War Game," I HEARD A SCREAM IN THE
STREET. Ed., Nancy Larrick. New York: Dell, 1970 (ages
10-adult).

     Allan Richards mourns the killing of children.

257. Richards, Laura E. FLORENCE NIGHTINGALE: THE ANGEL OF
THE CRIMEA: A STORY FOR YOUNG PEOPLE. New York: D. Appleton,
1915, 167 pp. (ages 12-16)

     Though a patronizing tone and quaint dialogue flaw this
version, the biography is nevertheless a decent rendition of
Florence Nightingale and the hospital situation during the
Crimean War. However, Ruth Fox Hume's biography is more
readable.

258. Richter, Hans P. FRIEDRICH. Translated by Edite Kroll.
New York: Holt, Rinehart and Winston, 1970, 149 pp. (ages
10-adult).

     Told from the perspective of a German, non-Jewish boy,
this hard hitting novel details the effect of the rise of the
Nazi party in Germany and the increasing humiliation of the
Jewish people.
     The chronology at the end of the book of the rise of Nazi
Germany and its effects on the Jews offers a chilling second
blow. It is an excellent book, winner of the Mildred L.
Batchelder Award.

259. Richter, Hans P. I WAS THERE. Translated by Edite Kroll.
New York: Holt, Rhinehart and Winston, 1972, 205 pp. (ages
10-adult).

     Both I WAS THERE and FRIEDRICH are autobiogriphical
books. The introductory note in this one goes:

               I am reporting how I lived through that time and
               what I saw--no more. I was there. I was not
               merely an eyewitness. I believed--and I will
               never believe again.

     The first person narrator of the book and his two
friends, Heinz and Gunther, belong to the Hitler youth move-
ment--though Gunther is not as enthusiastic as the others.
They experience the frenzied growth of Nazism and eventually
serve in the German army. The ending leaves the reader with
Gunther plunging crazily into a barrage of gunfire and certain
death.
     As with FRIEDRICH, there is a Chronology, which in some
ways is more frightening in depicting the efficient, rapid
rise of the Nazis than the story itself. There is also a
chart of the Hitler Youth Organizations.

260. Ringi, Kjell. THE STRANGER. Illustrated by the author.
New York: Random House, 1968, 31 pp. (ages 3-8).

     With his marvelous "childlike" illustrations and a few

simple sentences, Kjell Sorensen-Ringi presents the story of
the arrival of a giant stranger in the land of tiny people.
Frightened by this giant, the tiny people escalate their
efforts to get him to leave, finally shooting him with a
cannon. This, though hardly enough to hurt him physically,
causes him to cry, which floods the land, until the people
float to the level of his face, where they make friends with
him. It is a simple, symbolic plea for "communication" before
"confrontation."

261. Ringi, Kjell. THE WINNER. Illustrated by the author. New
York: Harper and Row, 1969, 30 pp. (ages 3-9).

     This wordless picture book pits two baby-like looking
people in a battle of one-upmanship. They face each other on
facing pages and continue to put on ever more elaborated cos-
tumes, until one, dressed as a dragon, eats the other. It is
an obvious symbolic presentation of the ultimate absurdity of
competition.

262. Roberts, Margaret. STEPHANIE'S CHILDREN. London: Victor
Gollanca, 1969, 208 pp. (ages 3-9).

     In a story about surviving the terrors of the French
Revolution, Margaret Roberts presents Stephanie, an eighteen-
year-old widower with two step-daughters. The story follows
the three of them as they struggle to escape and survive the
horrors of the Reign of Terror, eventually making their way to
London.
     The characters are fully developed, and the setting is
vividly described.
     According to Gillian Avery, who wrote a short "Intro-
duction" to the story, it was originally published anonymously
in 1896 "by the author THE ATELIER DU LYS," who was Margaret
Roberts, a little remembered writer born in 1833 and the author of at least thirty-eight books. Avery feels that this
author deserves more attention, being a writer "of unfailingly
high quality . . . [whose books are] head and shoulders above
most of her contemporaries."
     This books suggests that Margaret Roberts does, indeed,
deserve greater attention.

263. Rogers, Ingrid, ed. SWORDS INTO PLOWSHARES: A COLLECTION
OF PLAYS ABOUT PEACE AND SOCIAL JUSTICE. Elgin, Illinois:
Brethren Press, 1983, 281 pp. (ages 12-adult).

     This collection of twenty-seven skits and one-act plays
related to peace and social justice was gathered according to
the following criteria:

          The plays had to be selected to fit the needs
          not of a specific denomination, but rather of any
          group of people who desired to be introduced to,
          confronted with, or reinforced in Christ's message
          of peace. These then were the criteria which
          determined the choice:

Artistic beauty was important, but secondary to educational purpose.

2. Since the plays would be performed in churches, on the street, or at peace gatherings, we needed plays with fairly unsophisticated stage technology, simple dialogue, and clearly discernible message.

3. Last but not least, the plays had to be faith-centered, I mean by that not necessarily religious terminology or phrases within the play, but rather a set of ideas rooted in the Bible and Christ's teachings. . . .

Each play, then, is a fairly simple, straight forward presentation of a Christian virtue, suitable for performance in churches, schools, and community functions.

264. Rosenblatt, Roger. CHILDREN OF WAR. New York: Anchor Press/Doubleday, 1983, 212 pp. (ages 14-adult).

TIME magazine senior writer Roger Rosenblatt was sent on a 40,000 mile journey to collect data and put together a story for the magazine about children growing up in the world's war zones: Belfast, Israel, Lebanon, Cambodia, and Vietnam. The resulting story appeared in TIME, January 11, 1982. This book is based on that article, with several additions.
It is well written journalism, augmented with numerous philosophical insights, blunt (i.e., "And when the Israeli forces approached, one of the terrorists picked up the girl Einat by the feet and cracked open her head on a rock," p. 58) and yet filled with positive, sensitive hope (i.e., "'Yet here, among the children, I have been so moved and impressed by how wonderfully they are doing. I'm amazed how loving, how compassionate they can be.'" This statement was made by Neil Boothby, who arranged for the author to meet with children at the Children's Center in Khao I Dang, Cambodia, p. 142.).
The book won the 1984 Robert F. Kennedy Book Award and was nominated for the 1983 National Book Critics Circle Award. A number of black-and-white pictures are included. There is no bibliography.
It is a valuable book for introducing older children and adults to the realities of children living in a war situation.

265. Ross, Alan. "Radar," DON'T FORGET TO FLY. Collected by Paul Janeczko. New York: Bradbury, 1981. (ages 10-adult).

Extremely sensitive instruments destroy an enemy, bringing into question the responsibility of the operator.

266. Roth, Dan. "War," p. 71, REFLECTIONS ON A GIFT OF WATERMELON PICKLE . . . AND OTHER MODERN VERSE. New York: Lothrop, Lee & Shepard, 1967, 139 pp. (ages 10-adult).

This brief poem (21 words) juxtaposes war and nature through the personification of Dawn.

267.   Rottmann, Larry and Jan Barry and Basil T. Paquet, ed.
WINNING HEARTS & MINDS: WAR POEMS BY VIETNAM VETERANS. New
York: McGraw-Hill, 1972, 118 pp. (ages 12-adult).

The editors have arranged these poems by Vietnam veterans
"as a series of shifting scenes which describe, in rough
chronological order, a tour of combat duty in S. E. Asia,"
chronicling the "GIs' growing emotional and moral involvement
with the people and the land."
In addition to the poems, there are many black-and-white
drawings and photographs—though no credit is given for
photographers and illustrators. In general, the poetry is
more important as social documentation than as quality poetry.

268.   Rubin, Arnold P. THE EVIL THAT MEN DO: THE STORY OF THE
NAZIS. New York: Julian Messner, 1977.

This is a solid factual history of the regime of the
Nazis, centering on anti-Semitism, raising questions of guilt
(suggesting that apathy is a form of guilt), and alerting us
all to the lessons to be learned.
The title comes from a line by William Shakespeare, "The
evil that men do lives after them, the good is oft interred
with their bones," and the final lines of the book state that
"the time has come to reverse that statement," for "we have no
other choice." Considering the destructive potential of
nuclear weapons, the statement now takes on an even more
dramatic meaning.
A bibliography of other books dealing with Nazism is
included.

269.   Ryan, Cheli Duran. PAZ. Illustrated by Nonny Hopgrogian.
New York: MacMillan, 1971, 40 pp. (ages 5-7).

This picture book in simple lines and a few light colors
is apparently aimed at younger children, though the words are
difficult, at times, including some foreign names, and often
fill an entire page.
The pacifist Paz family lives half in France and half in
Spain. When the two countries declare war on one another, the
family decides to become a neutral country. Soon the soldiers
and others from both of the warring countries are living at
Paz, and the Paz family is finding it hard to feed the new
inhabitants. The Paz family says they will become French and
Spanish once again, if the two countries will declare peace.
Peace is declared.
The book expresses a simple, humorous, practical claim
that peace is better than war, though the highly improbable
circumstances and solution carry little force.
Children might find the story amusing, but may be mislead
about the true horror of war and the difficulty of ending it.

270.   Sachs, Marilyn. A POCKET FULL OF SEEDS. Illustraded by
Ben F. Stahl. New York: Doubleday, 1973, 137 pp. (ages 9-12).

Marilyn Sachs has written an excellent story based on the
real life of Fanny Bienstock Krieger (named Nicole in the
book), a twelve-year-old Jewish girl living in Aix-les Bains

during World War II. In 1943, Fanny's parents and sister are
taken by Nazi soldiers. She happens to not be at home at the
time and is left behind. The book both begins and ends with
her waiting anxiously to find out what happened to her family.
In between, it flashes back to the earlier war years to fill
in a realistic portrayal of what it was like to be Jewish in
France in World War II.

Nicole's character is convincingly drawn, the atmosphere
of the time and place is well presented, and the horror and
hatred for the Jews is subtly brought into an uneasy and
unresolved conclusion.

The black-and-white illustrations extend the story,
though it can stand on its own.

271.   Samuels, Gertrude. MOTTELE: A PARTISAN ODYSSEY. New
York: Harper and Row, 1976, 181 pp. (ages 12-adult).

This documentary novel follows the actions of a real
group of Jews who fought back against Hitler's regime. The
central character, Mottele, orphaned, joins a group of Jewish
partisians under Uncle Misha, and because of his Nordic looks,
is able to perform dangerous missions.

It is a good read for mature children, both on the level
of story, with fully realized characters, and as a thoroughly
researched presentation of Jewish resistance to Nazism.

An "Author's Note" at the beginning gives background
information, and an "Epilogue" gives Captain Misha's reply to
Hitler after the war:

> I, Moses, the son of Asher Halevi, have outlived
> you, after you condemned me to death. The Jewish
> people live!

272.   Sandberg, Carl. ABE LINCOLN GROWS UP. Reprinted from
ABRAHAM LINCOLN: THE PRAIRIE YEARS. Illustrated by James
Daugherty. New York: Harcourt Brace Jovanovich, 1926; Rpt.,
1953, 222 pp. (ages 10-15).

This contains the first twenty-seven chapters of
Sandburg's original two-volume biography and many excellent
black-and-white illustrations by James Daugherty (who has a
book of his own on Lincoln). It states in a "Publisher's Note"
at the beginning, the reason for leaving out the rest of
Sandburg's original biography is that young boys and girls are
less likely to be interested in Lincoln's political life.

Sandburg presents Lincoln as an impoverished boy eager
for books and knowledge, ambitious, and questioning:

> It seemed that Abe made the books tell him more
> than they told other people. . . . Abe picked out
> questions . . . such as "Who has the most right to
> complain, the Indian or the Negro?" and Abe would
> talk about it up one side and down the other.

Both the writing and the illustrations are excellent; for
older youth and adults, Sandburg's other writings on Lincoln
are highly recommended, especially: ABRAHAM LINCOLN: THE
PRAIRIE YEARS (1926), the basis of this book; ABRAHAM LINCOLN:
THE WAR YEARS (1939), a four volume set, winner of the

Pulitzer prize; and ABRAHAM LINCOLN (1954).

273. Sender, Roth Minsky. THE CAGE. New York: MacMillan, 1986, 245 pp. (ages 14-adult).

A horrifying account of the terrors of the Nazi concentration camps, this painfully true story will be emotionally hard reading, but the courage, love, and strength of spirit it reveals make it worth the effort.

274. Seredy, Kate. THE WHITE STAG. Illustrated by the author. New York: Viking Press, 1937, 95 pp. (ages 10-15).

Kate Seredy is a highly respected writer/illustrator of books for middle aged children, praised for the depiction of vitality and charm in her illustrations, especially noted for her illustrations of horses.
This powerful presentation of Attila (seen, perhaps, for the first time by Western children as a heroic character) is told as if it were a myth or an epic. The illustrations are in soft shades of black-and-white and have a forceful three-dimensional quality. They are extremely well done.
It is a historical Hungarian tale about the journeys and exploits of many great leaders of that heritage, mainly relating the legend of the separation of the Huns and the Megyars. It offers a strong picture of the mighty warrior Attila, and expresses a feeling of pride and faith in the Hungarian heritage. Kate Seredy claims to have written the book in three weeks, almost as if it had come out of her "tribal memory" (she was born in Hungary).
It received the Newbery Medal in 1938.

275. Serraillier, Ian. THE CHALLENGE OF THE GREEN KNIGHT. Illustrated by Victor G. Ambrus. New York: Henry Z. Walck, 1967, 56 pp. (ages 8-12).

This is a shortened retelling of SIR GAWAIN AND THE GREEN KNIGHT in a loose rhymed form with many archaic words.
Serraillier has written several such retellings of myths and epics for children, including: BEOWULF THE WARRIOR, 1961; ROBIN AND HIS MERRY MEN, 1970; and ROBIN IN THE GREENWOOD, 1968. These are generally good, spirited attempts to retain the original flavor while modernizing the language.

276. Serraillier, Ian. THE SILVER SWORD. Illustrated by C. Walter Hodges. New York: S. G. Phillips, 1956, 187 pp. (ages 9-16).

Four children travel from Poland to Switzerland to find their parents who have been taken away by the Nazis. It is a good book, based on a true story, realistic, but not as brutally realistic as many of these books about the Jewish Holocaust.

277. Seuss, Dr. THE BUTTER BATTLE BOOK. Illustrated by the author. New York: Random House, 1984, 42 pp. (ages 5-adult).

The Yooks, who eat their bread with the butter side up,
live on one side of "the wall"; the Zooks, who eat their bread
with the butter side down, live on the other. Both sides
guard the wall.

   The picture book begins with a grandfather taking his
grandson out to the wall to explain to him the history of the
"cold" conflict. Beginning with nothing more than simple
slingshots, the two sides got caught up in creating ever more
powerful weapons to outdo each other. The book ends with the
grandfather balancing precariously on the wall, along with a
grandfather from the other side; each holds the latest weapon
in his hand, the "Bitsy Big-Boy Boomeroo," a bomb no bigger
than a bean that can blow up all of the enemy in an instant.
The young boy calls out for his grandfather to be careful.
Everyone else has retreated into holes in the ground. It is
an obvious allegory of the arms race.

   While the book contains the same play with language and
illustrations that have delighted young children in Dr. Seuss
for years, there is a possible problem in structure.
Throughout most of the book, the grandfather is telling his
grandson the story, yet the story ends up with the grandfather
on the wall, proclaiming he is ready to ". . . make history! /
RIGHT HERE! AND RIGHT NOW!" The grandson replies: "Grandpa!"
I shouted. "Be careful! Oh, gee! / Who's going to drop it? /
Will YOU . . .? Or will HE . . .?" The grandfather speaks the
final words: "Be patient," said Grandpa. "We'll see. We
will see . . ."

   It is a dramatic, frightening climax. The problem is not
resolved, and in fact, at least on an initial reading,
immediate annihilation seems most likely.

   This makes for an exciting (and controversial) picture
book.

   However, in order to create this dramatic ending to this
allegory of cold war, Dr. Seuss has had to ignore (or
purposely juxtapose) that most of the story has been told by
the grandfather to his grandson in past tense (the book begins
"On the last day of summer / ten hours before fall . . . / .
. . my grandfather took me / out to the wall"). The story is
told in a leisurely fashion as something that has built up
over a long time period. However, the shift from past tense
to present tense takes place quickly (without time for the
lengthy discussion, the grandfather's telling of the history
of the conflict to his grandson, that makes up the major
portion of the picture book, preceding it).

   When does/did the grandfather calmly tell his grandson
the history of the arms build-up? If he did it before his
dramatic rush to the wall, some of it could not have been
included. If he did it after his balancing act on the wall,
then, of course, the immediate dramatic possibility of blowing
up the world must have been resolved, since both grandfather
and grandson were alive at a later date. Though, obviously,
it is legitimate to shift to present tense in literature for
dramatic emphasis, and though that is being done here, that
alone does not justify Dr. Seuss's possible flaw in logic.
Rather (unless one assumes an oversight), it must be assumed
that Dr. Seuss is emphasizing by purposely mixing tenses and
narrators that if the Bitsy Big-Boy Boomeroo (nuclear weapons)
ever were **dropped** there would be no one left to tell the

story.
          THE BUTTER BATTLE BOOK is a good book, a humorous,
imaginative presentation, in simple terms, of the current
situation between the United States and Russia. Children may
not be able to understand all the complexities of the arms
race, but they can relate to the absurdity of the battle
between the Yooks and the Zooks and how it relates to the
"bigger, better, best" mentality. In this book, children see
adults behaving like children, bad children at that. A fun
book (filled with clever word play and illustrations) has
taught a lesson which either immediately or in the future
children can apply to the nuclear arms race.
          Unfortunately, many librarians, apparently because of the
obvious allegory, have placed the book in the adult sections
of their libraries. The book can be read on at least two
levels, as many important critics of children's literature
have pointed out might serve as a criterion of good children's
literature (think of the possible levels fairy tales can be
read on), and one of those levels might be considered an adult
level, but that seems a strange reason for depriving children
of enjoying the book on one level (it would be sad to see the
same logic used to deprive children of reading fairy tales),
even if the second level is beyond them--which might not be
the case.
          Several other recent picture books fit into this same
controversial category, i.e., HIROSHIMA NO PIKA, WOLF OF
SHADOWS, and ROSE BLANCHE.

278.   Sherwood, Kate Brownlee. "Molly Pitcher"; rpt., p. 183,
THE GOLDEN TREASURY OF POETRY. Edited by Louis Untermeyer.
Illustrated by Joan Walsh Anglund. New York: Golden Press,
1959, 324 pp. (all ages).

          Kate Brownlee Sherwood tells how Molly Pitcher jumped to
replace her killed husband as a bombardier while fighting the
British at Monmouth.

279.   Siegal, Aranka. UPON THE HEAD OF A GOAT: A CHILDHOOD IN
HUNGARY, 1939-1944. New York: Farrar, Straus and Giroux, 1981,
184 pp. (ages 12-adult).

          Based on Aranka Siegal's own experiences as a child in
Hungary during the Holocaust, the story details Piri David-
owitz's survival, through both courage and luck, of the Nazi
regime.
          The title comes from Leviticus 16:

               And the Lord said unto Moses ". . . Aaron shall
          lay both his hands upon the head of the live
          goat, and confess over him all the inequities of
          the children of Israel, and all their transgres-
          sions, even all their sins; and he shall put them
          upon the head of the goat, and shall send him a-
          way by the hand of an appointed man into the
          wilderness.

          It is one of many excellent books about a child living
through (or in some cases dying in) the Holocaust, i.e., ALAN
AND NAOMI by Myron Levoy; THE UPSTAIRS ROOM by Johanna Reiss;

WHEN HITLER STOLE PINK RABBIT by Judith Kerr. and FRIEDRICH by
Hans Peter Richter.
    There are also several good guides for dealing with this
literature in a class room setting, i.e., FACING HISTORY AND
OURSELVES: HOLOCAUST AND HUMAN BEHAVIOR by Margot Stern Strom
and William S. Parsons.

280. Sharmat, Marjorie Weinman. I'M NOT OSCAR'S FRIEND
ANYMORE. Illustrated by Tony DeLuna. New York: E. P. Dutton,
1975, 28 pp. (ages 4-6).

    A boy decides not to be Oscar's friend anymore and thinks
up all the bad things he can about Oscar, but then decides to
call Oscar and be friends again.

281. Singer, Isaac Bashevis. THE POWER OF LIGHT: EIGHT
STORIES FOR HANUKKAH. Illustrated by Irene Lieblich. New York:
Farrar, Straus, Giroux, 1980, 87 pp. (ages 8-adult).

    Master storyteller, Isaac Singer weaves his artistry
through eight miraculous Hanakkah tales, one a true tale of
the escape of David and Rebecca from Nazi Germany--the first
refugees to reach the Holy Land. It is a truly beautiful tale
of hope and love succeeding over tremendous odds wonderfully
told.
    There are several full color illustrations in a com-
bination realistic/impressionist style that present a child-
like accompaniment to the text--but it is the text that makes
the book.

282. Singer, Isaac Bashevis. WHY NOAH CHOSE THE DOVE.
Illustrated by Eric Carle. Translated by Elizabeth Shub. New
York: Farrar, Straus and Giroux, 1974, 28 pp. (ages 5-9).

    Isaac Singer tells of the bragging of the other animals
as they vied to be on Noah's ark. However, since the dove is
modest, Noah chooses it to be his messenger. The book ends:

        The dove lives happily with fighting. It is a
        bird of peace.

    Eric Carle offers his usual bright, bold pictures.

283. Slobodkin, Louis. WILBUR THE WARRIOR. Illustrated by the
author. New York: Vanguard Press, 1972, 40 pp. (ages 5-8).

    This picture book concerns the King of Bingland, a skinny
warrior always ready at a moment's notice to go forth and
defend his kingdom. However, after many years of success in
battle and feeling his kingdom was now safe from enemies,
Wilbur hung up his armor and began to try and amuse himself
with less physical pursuits (croquet, shuttlecock, dominoes)
and to nibble on sweets, until, of course, he became fat and
out of shape for battle. While this was happening, his gen-
erals realized that the enemies were becoming bolder, beginning to make raids upon the kingdom. At first, Wilbur simply
ignored the warnings. Then, when he did realize the danger,

he found that he was too fat for his armor and his horse was
too out of shape for battle. The enemies moved ever closer
and it looked as if the kingdom would be defeated. The King
paced and worried, finally "worrying" off his fat. In the
meantime, his horse went uncared for, and thus, also lost its
fat. Wilbur mounted his horse, defeated the enemy, and re-
stored the kingdom to its former status. From then on, the
book points out, King Wilbur stayed in shape.
        The illustrations are sketchy line drawings, cartoon
style, with some sloppy water colors (very carelessly drawn).
The story itself is apparently played for laughs; for example,
it begins:

> A long, long time ago, before people were
> Republicans or Democrats (or whatever they want to
> be), when the world was ruled by kings and queens
> or people like that, the bravest ruler in all the
> world was the slender young King of Bingland.

        If there is a message, it is that a country must remain
constantly ready for battle to defend itself, and if prepared
will rather easily defeat the enemy (nameless encroachers).

284. Snow, Richard. FREELON STARBIRD: BEING A NARRATIVE OF
THE EXTRAORDINARY HARDSHIPS SUFFERED BY AN ACCIDENTAL SOLDIER
IN A BEATEN ARMY DURING THE AUTUMN AND WINTER OF 1776.
Illustrated by Ben F. Stahl. New York: Haughton, 1976, 209 pp.
(ages 12-adult).

        This American Revolution novel, told by Freelon Starbird
as an old man looking back and trying to make sense out of his
involvement in it, offers an ironic view of it, focusing on
the practical hardships (cold, lack of clothes, lack of supplies, dysentery) rather than its nobility, which Freelon
seems to only half understand and care about. The detail is
excellent. The perspective makes it better for older, mature
youth.

285. Sone, Monica. NISEI DAUGHTER. Boston: Little, Brown,
1953, 238 pp. (ages 12-adult).

        Kazuko (meaning peace) Monica (after St. Monica), a
Japanese girl and her family, living in Seattle, experience
the racism of World War II--Japanese concentration camps,
relocation, and so on. At first, she is ashamed about her
Japanese blood, feels as if she has two heads (one Japanese
and one American), but later learns to be proud of both.
        The book is filled with humor and warmth, rather than
despair and frustration--a book of smiling courage.

286. Speare, Elizabeth George. THE BRONZE BOW. Boston:
Houghton Mifflin, 1961, 266 pp. (ages 10-adult).

        The title comes from the Song of David:

> He trains my hands for war
> So that my arms can bend a bow of bronze.

It is about Daniel, who, filled with hatred, joins the
underground group that fights to "bend the bronze bow" of
Rome. When he meets Jesus, however, and finds Jesus embracing
love rather than hate for the enemy, Daniel's own hate begins
to leave him.

Though the book is pious and contrived, it does introduce
children to Jesus' doctrine of peace as opposed to war.

287. Steele, William O. THE PERILOUS ROAD. Illustrated by
Paul Galdone. New York: Harcourt, Brace & World, 1958, 191 pp.
(ages 8-12).

Eleven-year-old Chris Brabson lives on Walden's Ridge,
and thinks it the finest place in creation, that is, until the
Yankee devils arrive. The first thing they do is steal his
new hunting shirt from Silas, who had taken the leather to his
sister to have it sewed up right so Chris could surprise his
family. Chris decides right then and there he is going to
make some Yank pay for it.

Then, Yankee soldiers loot his families cabin. Chris is
furious, wants to start shooting. But forty-year-old Silas
holds him back. Then, Chris gets a shock--his brother Jethro
tells him he is on the Yankee's side. In fact, the Yanks had
paid for the food Chris thought they were stealing. And what
is worse, his "pappy" understands Jethro's decision to go and
fight for the Yanks. Now the neighbors turn against the
family, and Chris has to suffer for Jethro's decision.

Chris gets pushed by Lukie to prove he is for the South,
and though Lukie chickens out at the last minute, Chris
follows through on a plan to let out all the mules at a Yankee's camp. He nearly gets caught. But Silas, who apparently was following him, saves him and brings him home.

But then, Lukie's father and some other neighbors, including Silas, set the families' shed on fire. When Chris
confronts him, Silas says he only pretended to help burn the
shed, says he really went along to help keep the others from
doing even worse. Chris then decides that Silas is a spy,

Chris decides to help Silas. So when he sees an army of
Yankees moving through, he runs and reports it to Silas, so
Silas can tell the Confederates. But then, later, Chris
learns that his brother Jethro might be among that army--that
he, Chris, might be the cause of Jethro's death.

Chris sneaks out to the Yankee's camp to warn Jethro,
can't find Jethro, because, as he later learns, Jethro is
still in boot camp, but Chris ends up "liking" the Yankees.
Then the Confederate army attacks (even shooting at Chris).
Chris, at first, thinks it's all his fault. He later learns
it isn't, that Silas is nothing more than a lying good-for-
nothing.

Chris has learned that the war and the soldiers are, as
his father has tried to tell him, simply a bad thing, sad for
both sides.

The thrust of the action, obviously, comes from continual
misunderstanding on Chris's part, but ultimately, it does tie
in with the theme of war as misunderstanding.

Paul Gladone has done several realistic line drawings of
decent quality.

Steele is a prolific writer about the American frontier,
most of his books presenting the struggles of the early settlers from the white man's perspective. All of his work is

highly researched.

288.   Steele, William O. THE WAR PARTY. Illustrated by Lovinda
Bryan Cauley. New York: Harcourt Brace Jovanovich, 1978, 64
pp. (ages 3-6).

     William O. Steele has written numerous books for children
(THE PERILOUS ROAD was a Newbery Medal Honor Book in 1959) and
is noted for his vivid portrayal of frontier life. In this
"Let Me Read" book for young readers he tells the story of a
young Indian's first battle, one he has looked forward to as a
time of glory. However, the boy experiences something different in the battle, as people are hurt and killed and he
watches a young boy, exactly like him, on the other side get
killed. As he lies badly wounded, he realizes that war is not
filled with glory so much as it is filled with suffering and
death.
     The illustrations in black-and-white by Bovinda Bryan
Cauley are excellent realistic depictions of the Native
American life style and the horrors of war.
     A glossary is included to define unfamiliar terms. All
in all, this is an excellent book for introducing young
readers to the harsh realities of war.

289. Steichen, Edward. THE FAMILY OF MAN: THE GREATEST
PHOTOGRAPHIC EXHIBITION OF ALL TIME--503 PICTURES FROM 68
COUNTRIES--CREATED BY EDWARD STEICHEN FOR THE MUSEUM OF MODERN
ART. New York: Maco Magazine, Corp., 1955, 192 pp. (all ages).

     This is a marvelous "National Geographic" type of black-
and-white photographic essay, covering the entire human experience from birth to death throughout the globe--including
thought provoking photographs on war.
     Carl Sandberg has written a poignant prologue and many of
the pages include brief, to-the-point quotations from famous
people throughout history and across cultures.

290.   Steig, William. THE BAD ISLAND. Illustrated by the
author. New York: Simon and Schuster, 1969, 30 pp. (ages
3-10).

     Master picture book writer/illustrator William Steig has
created a parable about ugly and beauty, hate and love, war
and peace. The Bad Island is filled with evil, hateful
creatures who are constantly at war with one another. Suddenly, a flower appears. The creatures are suspicious, blame
one another, eventually annihilate each other. The flowers
spread, and the island becomes an uninhabited paradise. The
full color illustrations are excellent.

291.   Stein, R. Conrad. THE STORY OF D-DAY. Illustrated by Tom
Dinnington. Chicago: Children's Press, 1977, 32 pp. (ages
5-8).

     This book, one of a series of "Cornerstones of Freedom"
books, offers a very pro-American description of the happen-

ings of the Battle of Normandy, June 6, 1944.

It ends with the words from one of the signs currently standing near the cliffs of Pointe du Hoc:

> HERE THE WARRIORS SLEEP. THE CHAOS OF BATTLE HAS
> UNITED THEM FOR ETERNITY.

292. Stokes, Kathleen. MAID OF ORLEANS: THE STORY OF JOAN OF ARC. Illustrated by Marjorie Tomes. Boston: Bentley, 1953, 180 pp. (ages 10-16).

Drawing on Mark Twain's translation of the Sieur Louis de Conte's "Personal Recollections of Joan of Arc," Kathleen Stokes offers a straight forward version of Joan of Arc, not siding with or against Joan of Arc's claim to hear voices of St. Michael, St. Margaret, and St. Catherine (though the re-counting of Joan of Arc's belief, along with that of several superstitious women of the village, in the fairies of the tree and the bad fever Joan had as a child suggest she, after all, was not "really" hearing God's saints.

Nevertheless, whatever her source of belief and courage, she is presented here as a sensitive, brave, mistreated, and very admirable person.

The black-and-white illustrations are excellent.

293. Strieber, Whitley and James W. Kunetka. WARDAY AND THE JOURNEY ONWARD. New York: Holt, Rinehart and Winston, 1984, 374 pp. (ages 14-adult).

October 28, 1988, Warday, the Soviet Union launches a surprise nuclear attack on the United States, destroying Washington, D.C., San Antonio and the eastern edge of Queens, leaving Manhattan in ruins, and detonating smaller bombs over Minuteman and MX missile sites across the northern plains. Five years later, Whitley and Jim (the two novelists, writing as if they were there) set out to report on the condition of America.

Filled with extensive details (Government documents, fallout maps, surveys, and transcripts of interviews with survivors, including doctors and elected officials), the text presents itself as a journalistic report of an actual event.

It is a good (better than the television show, "The Day After") supposition of what life might be like after a nuclear war.

Whitley Strieber has written a book on the aftermath of a nuclear war for younger children, WOLF OF SHADOWS, that is excellent. James W. Kunetka has written several books for adults on the subject, including CITY OF FIRE: LOS ALAMOS AND THE ATOMIC AGE and OPPENHEIMER: THE YEARS OF RISK.

294. Strieber, Whitley. WOLF OF SHADOWS. New York: Alfred A. Knopf, 1985, 105 pp. (ages 7-adult).

This excellent book about the bond that forms between a human woman and a wolf following a nuclear holocaust presents a view of wolves (animals and nature in general) that comes, at least partially, from the Native American views of nature and man as all of one piece.

The book attempts to "see" through the eyes of the wolf,
and offers a wonderful commentary on the humans' loss of unity
with nature and their use of guns and violence to solve all
their problems. At the same time, it carries with it a more
peaceful vision, one that any creature determined to build
bigger and better weapons of destruction has obviously lost.

Though it deals with nuclear holocaust and violence on
lesser levels, the tone of it and comfortable alternate view
make it good reading for younger children.

295. Suhl, Yuri. ON THE OTHER SIDE OF THE GATE. New York:
Franklin Watts, 1975, 151 pp. (ages 12-adult).

Yuri Suhl, who has written other books dealing with the
Jewish situation during the Holocaust, has based this story on
a real-life incident. Two Jews, Hershel and Lena Bregman in
the story, in Poland have been confined to a Jewish ghetto
with the rest of the town's Jews. Pregnancy is outlawed.

However, Lena, through the secret help of others, gives
birth to David, and the story follows their task of smuggling
him out of the ghetto.

It is a story of Christians and Jews working together to
foil the inhuman actions of the Nazis--a story of the human
will to survive.

296. Suhl, Yuri. UNCLE MISHA'S PARTISANS. New York: Four
Winds Press, 1973, 211 pp. (ages 10-18).

By the author of THEY FOUGHT BACK: THE STORY OF JEWISH
RESISTANCE IN NAZI EUROPE (a documentary), this book, cen-
tering on the orphan Mottele, presents an instance of active
Jewish resistance (a topic seldom brought to light) in the
Ukraine during World War II.

Based on a true even, it is a blunt portrayal of the dark
side of war, and promotes revenge and, at least in certain
circumstances, violence.

297. Sutcliff, Rosemary. THE CAPRICORN BRACELET. Illustrated
by Richard Cuffari. H.Z. Walck, 1973, 149 pp. (ages 14-adult).

Rosemary Sutcliff is a highly respected, prolific writer
of generally hard reading historical fiction, most of it dealing with the history of early England, and the occupation of
the country by Norsemen, Romans, Normans, and Saxons.

She is always highly praised for her tremendous detail
and historical accuracy (sometimes condemned for too much
detail). She is also praised for the depth of her themes
(often dealing with the birth and growth and endurance of a
community, and with various individual qualities, freedom,
loyalty, rebirth, etc.).

In this book, the Calpurnius family experiences the
withdrawl of Roman power from Scotland. The battle scenes
(standard in her fiction) are vividly brought to life. If
there is any great flaw, it is that the characters are a bit
too sure of themselves (they could have more inner struggle).

As mentioned, Sutcliff is a prolific writer. This was
her thirtieth publication. Including a rewrite of BEOWULF,

and several other works on English history, many of her books,
in addition to this one, deal with war. Some of them are discussed in the following entries:

298. Sutcliff, Rosemary. DAWN WIND. Illustrated by Charles
Keeping. H. Z. Walck, 241 pp. (ages 11-15).

    DAWN WIND follows the Saxon invasion of sixth century
Britain through the adventures of Owain, a British farmer's
son, sole survivor of the battle with the Saxons at Aquae
Sulis, and Regina, who he cares for. As always in her writing, it is filled with historical details.

299. Sutcliff, Rosemary. THE EAGLE OF THE NINTH. Illustrated
by C. Walter Hodges. London: Oxford, 1954, 225 pp. (ages
11-15).

    A young centurion's quest for his father serves as the
center for a look at the Roman occupation of Britain.

300. Sutcliff, Rosemary. HEROS AND HISTORY. Illustrated by
Charles Keeping. New York: Putnam, 1966, 152 pp. (ages 11-18).

    Sutcliff presents detailed pictures of ten of England's
best known heros in action: Caratacus, Arthur, Alfred, Here-
ward, Llewellin, Robin Hood, William Wallace, Robert the
Bruce, Owen Glyndwri, and Montrose.

301. Sutcliff, Rosemary. KNIGHT'S FEE. Illustrated by Charles
Keeping. H. Z. Walck, 1960, 241 pp. (ages 11-18).

    Here she offers a story of knighthood in the middle ages
in the form of two friends. Randal becomes a squire (compan-
ion) to a young English noble and is initiated into the world
of knighthood during the time of the Norman Conquest.

302. Sutcliff, Rosemary. THE LANTERN BEARERS. Illustrated by
Charles Keeping. H. Z. Walck, 1965, 305 pp. (ages 11-18).

    This is another of Sutcliff's stories of the Roman
occupation of Britain, once again filled with authentic
details and evocative scenes--one of her best.
    Aguila, the main character, let his troop sail without
him when the Romans left Britain, and suffered much, as the
Saxons killed his father, stole his sister, and made him a
thrall, etc.

303. Sutcliff, Rosemary. THE MARK OF THE HORSE LORD. H. Z.
Walck, 1965, 305 pp. (ages 11-18).

    A novel of the coming of age--filled with well written
battle scenes--set in Scotland, 2nd century, this tells the
struggle of Phaedrus, a Roman gladiator-slave. Since he looks
like the lost prince of a western Scottish tribe, he becomes
the Horse Lord of the Dalriadain, and thus the leader of a
group sworn to overthrow the evil rule of a woman who has

usurped the throne.
     It is a dark, difficult novel.

304.   Sutcliff, Rosemary. OUTCAST. Illustrated by Richard
Kennedy. London: Oxford, 1955, 229 pp. (ages 11-18).

     Another book set during the Roman occupation of Britain--
this one is about Beric, who suffers deeply before coming
through tremendous ordeals.
     Beric is the baby son of a Roman soldier and is the only
survivor of a wrecked ship on the shore of Britain. He is rejected by both Britain and Rome.
     It is a dark, difficult read.

305.   Sutcliff, Rosemary. RIDER ON A WHITE HORSE. New York:
McCann, 1960, 320 pp. (ages 11-18).

     Anne Fairfax rides into the English Civil Wars with her
husband and daughter in seventeenth century England.

306.   Sutcliff, Rosemary. THE SILVER BRANCH. Illustrated by
Charles Keeping. London: Oxford, 1958, 215 pp. (ages 11-18).

     This is a tale of third century Roman Britain, which
concerns itself with the theme of the future of Britain and
the detailed rendering of the political and military picture
of the times. After the murder of Carausius (ruler of Britain), Justin and Flavius go underground to serve Rome.

307.   Sutcliff, Rosemary. SIMON. Illustrated by Richard
Kennedy, 1953; rpt. London: Oxford, 1979, 257 pp. (ages
14-adult).

     This is a well written tale of the English Civil War,
1642-1660, and the friendship of two boys. As is a tendency
in her writing, it becomes a bit cluttered with battle scenes.

308.   Sutcliff, Rosemary. WARRIOR SCARLET. Illustrated by
Charles Keeping. H. Z. Walck, 1958, 207 pp. (ages 12-16).

     A story of the Bronze Age (900 B.C.) in England--this
centers on Drem, presenting him as a strong, brave, fierce
young man.
     At first, he fails his test to wear the coveted Warrior
Scarlet (which is to kill a wolf single-handed) because of his
withered arm, but he later returns as a man and a warrior.

309.   Swindell, Robert. BROTHER IN THE LAND. Middlesex,
England: Oxford Univ. Press, 1984; rpt. New York: Viking
Penguin, 1985, 149 pp. (ages 12-18).

     Though consideration of the possibility of any form of
life after a nuclear war may seem optimistic, this book deals
bluntly with what life might be like after such a holocaust,

from the detailing of the grotesque scenes immediately following the bombing, filled with rubble and dead bodies, to the
subsequent struggle for life in a world without safe food or
water, where people are dying from radiation poisoning, setting up Nazi like concentration camps, and even participa-
ting in cannibalism.

The novel falls off towards the end, but it is, nevertheless, a good attempt to portray nuclear war and its after
effects.

310. Switzer, Ellen. HOW DEMOCRACY FAILED. New York:
Athenium, 1975, 176 pp. (ages 12-adult).

Written in response to the youth disallusionment with
America in the 1960s-1970s by a woman who lived through Nazi
Germany, this is an interesting non-fiction account (though
all the names have been changed), based on interviews con-
ducted in 1972-1973 with Germans who were teenagers during
World War II--some who were ardent Nazis.

It is a valuable book, worth reading.

311. Syme, Ronald. BENEDICT ARNOLD: TRAITOR OF THE
REVOLUTION. Illustrated by William Stobbs. New York: William
Morrow, 1970, 192 pp. (ages 8-12).

Prolific author of books for children, Ronald Syme
presents a sharp tempered, self-centered, self-made, extremely
intelligent, misunderstood and volatile Benedict Arnold.

Perhaps the best in-combat officer in te revolution,
Arnold could not handle the world in any other manner than by
his rash, forward, battle personality. His continual conflicts with all the other leaders of the revolution (except
Washington) eventually lead Arnold, in a bitter rejection of
the American Revolution, to become a traitor.

This biography (which includes passages from Arnold's
letters and some other correspondence of the time) presents a
man of action who, apparently, could only exist with bullets
in the air. There is a great deal of action and the excitement one would also find in a "Rambo" movie. Some time is
given to a contemplation of the rightness of Arnold's approach
to life; however, readers may miss the point--i.e., battle is
not glamorous. Readers will get a frantic picture of the
unorganized, confusing mess that accompanied the revolution.

312. Synder, Louis L. THE FIRST BOOK OF WORLD WAR II. New
York: Franklin Watts, 1958, 96 pp. (ages 8-12).

This is a simplified history of World War II (very pro
Allied Powers). It has several photographs (some of a graphic
nature), some maps, a brief list of World War II words with
definitions, and an Index.

313. Szambelan-Strevinsky, Christine. DARK HOUR OF NOON. New
York: J. B. Lippincott, 1982, 215 pp. (ages 10-adult).

A story of the children's underground resistance in

Poland during World War II, the book follows Trina Szumkowskis
as she is sent to an internment camp with her family, then to
a small apartment shared by two families, becomes involved
with the underground movement, and helps during the Polish
uprising of 1944.

As the prologue points out, beginning on Sept. 1, 1939,
when the German army started its rapid take over of Poland,
and extending some five years (during which time the SS li-
quidated many Jews in Lodz, Krakow, Radon, etc., and massacred
them in ghettos--the most infamous being Warsaw), until August
1, 1944, when the Polish people attempted to seize back Warsaw
in a disastrous uprising (The Polish Rising), the Polish (both
Christians and Jews) experienced the full force of Nazism.

Christine Szambelan-Strevinsky offers a detailed fiction
of that time, and of the children's experience within it.

314.   Takashima, Shichan. A CHILD IN PRISON CAMP. New York:
Morrow, 1974, 64 pp. (ages 7-12).

Shichan Takashima, currently a highly respected Canadian
artist, was born prematurely, which resulted in her being
small and having a slight limp all of her life. Her slow
physical development made her even more of a child during her
internment in the Japanese-Canadian prison camps during World
War II, which she recounts here in a fictionalized, though
honest portrayal. And it is this child-like innocence that
gives the book it's power.

The large size format of the book gives it a picture book
appearance, and it does have seven full color impressionist
pictures. However, the rest of the book is pure text on large
pages with a good deal of white space (large margins with
margin headings to let the reader know just where the text is
at, i.e., "Fall, 1943, High School for Yuki").

An afterword explains the reality the story is based on.
It is an excellent introduction to often overlooked aspect of
World War II.

315.   Thoreau, Henry David. "Civil Disobedience," WALDEN AND
CIVIL DISOBEDIENCE. Edited by Owen Thomas. Reviews and
Commentary by Ralph Waldo Emerson, et al. New York: Norton,
1966, 422 pp. (ages 16-adult).

"Civil Disobedience" establishes the basis for the modern
concept of passive resistance as the final option for the expression of the opinion of the minority (most spectacularly
demonstrated in the life of Mahatma Gandhi).

It was first delivered as a lecture at the Concord
Lyceam, February, 1848, and first appeared in print under the
title "Resistance to Civil Government" in AESTHETIC PAPERS,
1849, edited and published by Elizabeth P. Peabody, Boston.

It places the individual above the government and demands
of the individual that he or she not live by the motto "My
government--right or wrong" but, rather, take a stand against
the government when the government and the majority are wrong.
It isn't hard to imagine what Henry David Thoreau would have
thought of John F. Kennedy's famous statement: "Ask not what
your country can do for you; ask what you can do for your
country."

The essay concludes:

> The authority of government, even such as I am
> willing to submit to,--for I will cheerfully obey
> those who know and can do better than I, and in
> many things even those who neither know nor can do
> so well,--is still an impure one: to be strictly
> just, it must have the sanction and consent of the
> governed. It can have no pure right over my person
> and property but what I concede to it. The progress
> from an absolute to a limited monarchy, from a lim-
> ited monarchy to a democracy, is a progress toward
> a true respect for the individual. Is a democracy,
> such as we know it, the last improvement possible in
> government? Is it not possible to take a step fur-
> ther towards recognizing and organizing the rights
> of man? There will never be a really free and en-
> lightened State, until the State comes to recognize
> the individual as a higher and independent power,
> from which all its own power and authority are de-
> rived, and treats him accordingly. I please my-
> self with imagining a State at last which can af-
> ford to be just to all men, and to treat the in-
> dividual with respect as a neighbor; which even
> would not think it inconsistent with its own repose,
> if a few were to live aloof from it, not meddling
> with it, nor embraced by it, who fulfilled all the
> duties of neighbors and fellow-men. A State which
> bore this kind of fruit, and suffered it to drop
> off as fast as it ripened, would prepare the way
> for a still more perfect and glorious State, which
> also I have imagined, but not yet anywhere seen.

316. Tibbets, Albert B., ed. AMERICAN HEROS ALL: STORIES OF
OUR SERVICEMEN IN ACTION IN THE WARS OF THE UNITED STATES FROM
THE AMERICAN REVOLUTIONARY TO KOREA. Boston: Little Brown,
1966, 313 pp. (ages 12-adult).

This collection of short stories by major writers--
Stephen Crane, William Faulkner, Ambrose Bierce, et al--offers
an introduction to the fiction of some of America's greatest
writers on war. While the editor Albert Tibbets claims to
admire all of the brave young men who fought for freedom, he
also expresses the hope that the United Nations will
accomplish its goal of peace on earth and goodwill among
nations.

317. Tolan, Stephanie S. PRIDE OF THE PEACOCK. New York:
Scribner, 1985, 185 pp. (ages 12-adult).

After reading Jonathan Schell's THE FATE OF THE EARTH,
fourteen-year-old Whitney Whitehurst becomes deeply despon-
dent, fearing the horrible likelihood of a nuclear holocaust.
By chance, she becomes a friend of Theodora Bush, a
famous sculptor who is grieving the murder of her husband.
The book follows them as they help each other overcome their
depressions.

The characters are well presented, and the relationship between them grows in a subtle manner.

318.   Tolkien, J. R. R. THE HOBBIT OR THERE AND BACK AGAIN, rev. ed. New York: Ballantine Books, 1982, 287 pp. (ages 10-adult); and THE LORD OF THE RINGS TRILOGY: Part I - THE FELLOWSHIP OF THE RING, 527 pp.; Part II - THE TWO TOWERS, 447 pp.; Part III - THE RETURN OF THE KING, 527 pp. New York: Ballantine Books, 1965. (ages 14-adult).

These four books, all comprising one story (though THE HOBBIT was written earlier and can stand on its own), present high fantasy at its best.
    The HOBBIT is the story of Bilbo Baggins, a comfort loving hobbit of Middle Earth who is drawn into helping thirteen dwarves in their expedition to Lonely Mountain to recover the treasure stolen years ago by the dragon Smaug.
    His challenges, adventures, and growth in this "quest" make up a wonderful fantasy (a version of the "hero myth" written about by Joseph Campbell and others).
    The trilogy chronicles the great War of the Ring in Middle Earth, and follows Frodo, as he and eight companions go on a journey to destroy the ring by casting it back into the fire from which it came.
    The four books offer a detailed other world, filled with all the elements of fantasy, where Good and Evil fight it out for control.
    For a clearer understanding of what he is trying to accomplish, readers should refer to J.R.R. Tolkien's famous essay, "On Fairy-stories," where he attempts to explain what high fantasy is and what it has to offer--stressing that fantasy, as opposed to many other forms of literature, gives us the "happy ending," the "eucatastrophe," a fleeting glimpse of "Joy"--which, for Tolkien, is a presentation of the Christian world view.

319.   Tsuchiya, Yukio.   FAITHFUL ELEPHANTS: A TRUE STORY OF ANIMALS, PEOPLE AND WAR, 1951; Translated by Tomoko Tsuchiya Dykes. Illustrated by Ted Lewin. Boston: Houghton Mifflin, 1988, 30 pp. (ages 8-adult.

This is one of several excellent picture books dealing with the use of nuclear weapons on Japan during World War II. In this case, it is the threat of the animals escaping during a nuclear attack (or even the dropping of standard bombs) that causes the tragedy.
    The story centers on the starving to death of three elephants at the Ueno Zoo in order to prevent that possibly dangerous situation. This simple logic is simply presented, and the horrible, sad result is offered in a straight forward story (a true story).
    Few will not be touched by the "necessary" and painful deaths of these elephants as the result of war. And since the story is well told and the illustrations are excellent, the only question will be the audience. Should or should not young children be exposed to such a distasteful side of the human condition?

320. Tunis, John R. SILENCE OVER DUNKERQUE. New York: William
Morrow, 1962, 215 pp. (ages 12-adult).

John R. Tunis is famous for his many well written sports
books for young adults. But here he tackles what it was like
to be marooned in Dunkerque, France, after the Battle of
France, 1940, As Tunis states, this is the story of "Sergeant
Edward Henry George Williams of the Second Battalion, The Wil-
shire Regiment, a prisoner of war in German hands."
     But Sergeant Williams really isn't a prisoner; rather, he
is stranded with Fingers, one of his men, and an adopted Airedale, that reminds him of his own Airedale Candy, in Dunkerque
during the German occupation.
     Of course (and the certainly of this suggests the pre-
dictability of the plot), he escapes and returns to his family
in England.
     It is an adventure story that teenage boys and, perhaps,
teenage girls (a young French girl helps Sergeant Williams
survive and escape), will enjoy. The plot is filled with
excitement and action. However, though war is not inten-
tionally glorified, it does come off as something of a
thrilling experience.

321. Tunis, John R. HIS ENEMY, HIS FRIEND. New York: William
Morrow, 1967, 196 pp. (ages 10-adult).

The "Author's Note" beginning the book claims that "This
is a book about the conscience of a man." It then goes on to
discuss the relationship between European football or soccer
and American football, and the reader may suspect that Tunis
is writing another of his popular sports books for young
adults. However, upon turn the page, the reader is immediately confronted with "Part I: Eve of Battle, June, 1944." So
just what is the book about: sports or war? Both and more.
The very first line of the "Note" proves to be the correct
answer.
     The book combines and separates the emotions that ac-
company sports and war, and it explores the deep human desire
for revenge. The need to win and the need to punish the foe,
mob violence and murder are all revealed. But there is another side--friendship, forgiving, risking one's life for an
enemy because it is wrong to kill out of hatred. This is an
excellent book and will be appreciated (and should be read) by
teenage boys (and men who have not yet grown-up).

322. Twain, Mark. THE WAR PRAYER. Originally published in
1921; Illustrated by John Groth. New York: Harper and Row,
1970, 82 pp. (ages 8-adult).

Albert Bigelow Paine, MARK TWAIN, A BIOGRAPHY, states:

          To Dab Beard, who dropped in to see him,
     Clemens read the "War Prayer," stating that
     he had read it to his daughter Jean, and
     others, who had told him he must not print
     it, for it would be regarded as sacrilege.
          "Still, you are going to publish it, are
     you not?"
          Clemens, pacing up and down the room in his

> dressing-gown and slippers, shook his head.
> "No," he said, "I have told the whole truth
> in that and only dead men can tell the truth in
> this world.
> It can be published after I am dead."

This poem by Mark Twain (Samuel Clemens), possibly
America's greatest writer, begins by recounting the surge of
patriotism in the country as the war begins ("It was a time of
great and exalting excitement."), moves to the Sunday morning
church service, which is filled with a calling upon God to
support and bless the "noble young soldiers" and make them
"invincible in the bloody onset." Everyone is excited, ready
for battle.
Then an old man in a robe appears and walks up the aisle.
He takes the place of the preacher and says "I come from the
Throne-- / bearing a message from Almighty God!" The assembly
is in shock. The stranger continues, saying that God has
heard and will grant the request, really two requests, one
spoken, one unspoken, made, but that first he must tell them
the unspoken part of the request. He then goes on to tell
them that in asking for a victory for their side they are also
asking for defeat (with its suffering and pain) for the other
side.
After the messenger leaves, the poem concludes with:

> It was believed afterward
> that the man was a lunatic,
> because there was no sense
> in what he said.

The drawings by John Groth, expressing the anguish of war
offer a decent accompaniment to the poem, but all in all, both
the drawings and the breaking up of the poem in this version
are more of a nuisance than a help. It is the poem itself
that carries the message. It should be required reading of
all high school students.

323. Uchida, Yoshiko. JOURNEY HOME. Illustrated by Charles
Robinson. New York: Atheneum, 1978, 131 pp. (ages 8-14).

This is the sequel to JOURNEY TO TOPAZ: A STORY OF
JAPANESE AMERICAN EVACUATION and should be read as a se-
quel--though it can stand on its own.
It recounts the struggles of Japanese-American Yuki
Sakane and her Mama, Papa, and brother Ken to rebuild their
lives after being released from an "alien" camp in Utah (Papa
had spent time in a camp in Montana), where they were interned
during World War II.
The psychological adjustments and emotional demands are
presented, as well as the physical hardships. It is an excellent book for introducing children (and adults) to a sad incident in American history.
The muted line drawings go well with the story.

324. Uchida, Yoshiko. JOURNEY TO TOPAZ: A STORY OF THE
JAPANESE-AMERICAN EVACUATION. Illustrated by Donald Carrick.
New York: Charles Scribner's Sons, 1971, 149 pp. (ages 8-14).

In the "Preface," Yoshiko Uchida explains how the story is based on her own experiences as a Japanese-American (one of 110,000 persons of Japanese ancestry indiscriminately uprooted and sent to internment camps as the result of an order issued by President Franklin D. Roosevelt, February, 1942, authorizing the Secretary of War to "prescribe areas from which any or all persons may be excluded"). In fact, Uchida states, "much of what happened to the Sakane family [the fictitious family in the book] also happened to my own."

This is a well written account revealing a seldom discussed "mistake" in America's past, a good introduction to the subject.

There are several well done black-and-white illustrations. For those who wish to follow the Sakane family's experiences readjusting to life after their internment, there is a sequel, JOURNEY HOME.

325.   Udry, Janice May. LET'S BE ENEMIES. Illustrated by Maurice Sendak. New York: Harper and Row, 1961, 28 pp. (ages 4-7).

James and John were best friends, but John had already built-up resentment toward James over numerous minor and/or imagined inconsiderate actions. John decided to tell James that he is now the enemy. However, as soon as he does, and James replies, they become friends again. The imagined thoughtlessness in never confronted.

The illustrations by Sendak, with his typical expressive facial expressions, capturing the emotions and thought of the two boys, are excellent.

326.   Untermeyer, Louis, ed. THE GOLDEN TREASURY OF POETRY. Illustrated by Joan Walsh Anglund. New York: Golden Press, 1959, 324 pp. (all ages).

This excellent collection of poetry includes several poems by highly respected poets on war and peace traditionally used in the classroom, for example: "Paul Revere's Ride," Henry Wordsworth Longfellow; "The Destruction of Sennacherib," Lord Byron; and "How They Brought the Good News from Ghent to Aix," Robert Browning. For a discussion of these poems, refer to their own entries.

327.   Van Stockum, Hilda. THE BORROWED HOUSE. New York: Farrar, Straus, Giroux, 1975, 215 pp. (ages 12-adult).

Janna is a member of the Hitler Youth Corp. They are learning and promoting the Aryan culture, and in training to become mothers of the great future race of German soldiers. Janna has already learned that the Aryan race is the master race by reading MEIN KAMPF and that the infiltration of the Christians (with their weak "Love Thy Enemy" ideas) and the Jews with their weak blood and strange communist ideas that are weakening the master race.

Janna's parents, the famous Mechtild and Otto Oster, have been travelling for over two years, entertaining troops in foreign countries Then, Aunt Hedwig, old and feeble, is taken away in an ambulance. Janna is worried, but an older boy,

standing next to her, tells her not to be concerned. Aunt
Hedwig is old and useless, a nuisance. And now is a time for
the youth to gather behind the nation about to enter a great
period.
     Shortly, Janna is united with her parents in Holland.
They and others have been given the house of the Van Arkels to
live in. Janna is even given the clothes of the Van Arkels'
girl.
     The house, it is hinted at (in a somewhat heavy-handed
manner), belonged to Jews. It also turns out that Janna's
mother does not share Janna and her father's dislike of Jews.
     Then Janna meets the Baron, friend of her mother, who has
arranged it all (the house, etc.) for the family, and who
Janna soon realizes has her mother's dangerous views about
Hitler.
     Later, Janna finds a secret room in the house and Sef Van
Gelder hiding in it, working to help the Jews. Janna's beliefs begin to change. She learns that the history she was
taught in the German schools was filled with lies. She begins
to fall in love with Sef, who she later realizes is a Jew.
Her parents have a fight over the Baron, who wants her mother
to run away with him. All this leads to a climatic conclusion—somewhat too melodramatic.
     The characters are full and the themes are important. It
offers an interesting perspective on the Holocaust.

328. Vigna, Judith. NOBODY WANTS A NUCLEAR WAR. Illustrated
by the author. Niles, Illinois: Albert Whitman & Company,
1986, 35 pp. (ages 4-8).

     A young girl and her brother decide to build a hideaway
just in case there is a nuclear war. After they do so, their
mother finds out about it and offers comfort, explaining very
briefly the beginning of nuclear war and giving positive ways
people are trying to prevent nuclear war. It is a simply told
story, meant to introduce children to the subject and give
them a non-threatening way of dealing with it.

329. Volavkova, Hana, ed. I NEVER SAW ANOTHER BUTTERFLY . . .
: CHILDREN'S DRAWINGS AND POEMS FROM TEREZIN CONCENTRATION
CAMP, 1942-1944. New York: McGraw-Hill, 1962, (all ages).

     This is a powerful book. It contains children's drawings
and poems from the Terezin concentration camp, a way station
to Oswiecim and other extermination centers. These children
were all condemned to die. They saw death and misery and
cruelty all around them, yet their poetry is more about the
joy of life than the fear of death. If reading this book
doesn't bring a tear to the eyes of the reader for the insane
cruelty humans are capable of then nothing will.
     The inside flap of the book cover states:

          The drawings and poems are all that is left of
          these children; their ashes have long since sifted
          across the fields around Oswiecim. Of those who
          signed their names to their work, it has been
          possible to find out a few facts: the year and
          place of their birth, the number of their trans-
          port to Terezin and to Oswiecim, and then the year

of their death. For most of them, it was 1944,
The next to the last year of World War II.

The poems were chosen from the archives of the State
Jewish Museum in Prague.

330. Wartski, Maureen Crane. A BOAT TO NOWHERE. See Maureen
Crane.

331. Wartski, Maureen Crane. A LONG WAY FROM HOME.
Philadelphia: Westminster Press, 1980, 155 pp. (ages
10-adult).

In this sequel to A BOAT TO NOWHERE, Kien, a fifteen-
year-old Vietnamese refugee, unable to adopt to his new home
in America and its prejudice, runs to a Vietnamese fishing
community, hoping he can "belong" there. After he helps the
people climb out from under Paul Orrin's evil ways, he decides
to return home, where he now feels welcome.

332. Watkins, Yoko Kawashima. SO FAR FROM THE BAMBOO GROVE.
New York: Lothrop, 1986, 183 pp. (ages 9-13).

Eleven-year-old Yoko tells how she and her family flee to
Seoul to escape the advance of the Korean Communist Army
during World War II. They live with death, suffering, and
violence in this realistically told story that also offers a
picture of the power of the human soul in the characters of
Yoko and her sister, Ko, and her mother.

333. Watson, Sally. HIGHLAND REBEL. Illustrated by Scott
Maclain. New York: Holt, 1954, 212 pp. (ages 9-12).

In 1745, Lauren Cameron waits for Bonnie Prince Charlie
to lead a rising against the English. She wishes she were a
boy, so she could wield a claymore for him. As it turns out,
her courage helps him in an escape. The descriptions of her
clothes, and so on, tend to suggest a female readership.

334. Watson, Sally. THE HORNET'S NEST. New York: Holt, 246
pp. (ages 12-16).

Ronald and Lauchlin McLeod flee persecution on the
Scottish Isle of Skye, only to encounter it once again in
Williamsburg in 1773. Employing an informal style, Sally
Watson reveals the events and mixed feelings that lead up to
the American Revolution.

335. Watson, Sally. THE MUKHTAR'S CHILDREN. New York: Holt,
Rinehart and Winston, 1968, 248 pp. (ages 12-adult).

Watson offers a thoroughly researched story of the early
days of the state of Israel. Mukhtar means village head.
Brief glossaries of Arabic and Hebrew are included.

336. Watson, Sally. OTHER SCANDALS. New York: Holt, 1966, 223
pp. (ages 12-adult).

    This thoroughly researched story details Devra Stutters
and her change from hating Arabs to the realization that life
is not that simple. It is a good, even-handed novel about the
Mideast War. Brief glossaries of Hebrew and Arabic terms are
included.

337. Watson, Sally. TO BUILD A LAND. Illustrated by Lili
Cassel. New York: Holt, 255 pp. (ages 10-14).

    Extremely noble European Jews fend off the Stern Gang as
they attempt to settle Israel just before the uneasy Israeli-
Arab truce.
    The descriptions of Isreal are vivid and clear and the
activities of the children, as they struggle to adjust to a
new life, read like high adventure.

338. White, Robb. DEATHWATCH. New York: Doubleday, 1972, 228
pp. (ages 12-16).

    Den, a decent man, narrates his battle against Madec, a
sadistic, evil man. They fight it out on an unnamed desert (a
standard good guy/bad guy facing-each-other-in-the-wild plot).
However, the ending, where Ben is not believed, offers a
twist. It is a fast paced adventure story.

339. White, Robb. THE FROGMEN. New York: Doubleday, 1973, pp.
240 (ages 12-15).

    Robb White, drawing on his own experiences in the navy,
has written several books dealing with war, some of which were
made into movies, and a number of screen plays and television
scripts, on the whole, adventure stories.
    This one centers on Amos Wainwright, an ensign assigned
to Chief Hingman in Underwater Demolition School. He and
friend John Nash, and others, then put their training to use
in disarming underwater Japanese mines operations in World War
II.
    It is filled with action, and the details reveal a know-
ledge of the subject matter. However, there is little in the
way of a theme.

340. White, Robb. SECRET SEA. Illustrated by Jay Hyde. New
York: Doubleday, 1947, 243 pp. (ages 12-adult).

    After World War II an ex-naval officer and a fifteen-
year-old boy seek Aztec gold on a Spanish ship sunk in the
Caribbean centuries earlier. A Nazi gang pursues them. As
always with White, the suspense, action, adventure take center
stage.

341. White, Robb. SILENT SHIP, SILENT SEA. New York:
Doubleday, 1967, 232 pp. (ages 12-adult).

Kelsey Devereux, a young seaman, and the captain of the
U.S. destroyer the Caron, a ship disabled by a Japanese plane,
struggle against one another as the ship is towed through the
Coral Sea by a Japanese ship. It is standard White adventure.

342. White, Robb. SURRENDER. New York: Doubleday, 1966, 239
pp. (ages 12-adult).

This story begins on Dec. 10, 1941, three days after the
bombing of Pearl Harbor, in the Philippine Islands. Juan and
Juanita Macquite, Filipino-American brother and sister are the
central characters, and their courage and endurance in the ugliness of this war from the Japanese attack on Pearl Harbor to
the surrender of the American forces at Bataan, reveal the human spirit at its highest.
Young teenagers will delight in the strength of spirit
evident in the midst of the horrors.
The exaggeration may be a bit too much, but the adventure
of it all should carry most readers beyond that flaw.

343. White, Robb. THE SURVIVOR. New York: Doubleday, 1964,
204 pp. (ages 12-15).

Adam Land doesn't want the secret World War II mission he
is assigned as a navy pilot, but changes, grows, as he is
cramped in a submarine with a select platoon of Marines on
route to gather information on a Japanese held island in the
South Pacific.
This novel is one of several action stories by Robb White
filled with suspense (and melodrama).

344. White, Robb. UP PERISCOPE. New York: Doubleday, 1960,
(ages 12-15).

Once again, Robb White offers an action packed top secret
mission aboard a submarine against the Japanese in World War
II. Lieutenant Keh Braden is smuggled ashore by submarine to
a Japanese held island for the purpose of stealing a Japanese
code.

345. Whitman, Walt. DRUM-TAPS, 1865, and SEQUEL TO DRUM-TAPS,
1865; poems from each reprinted in many contemporary anthol-
ogies (i.e., "When Lilacs Last in the Dooryard Bloom'd," THE
AMERICAN TRADITION IN LITERATURE. Vol. 2. Sculley Bradley,
Richmond Croom Beatty, and E. Hudson Long, ed. New York:
Norton, 1967. (ages 15-adult).

The highly respected nineteenth century American poet,
Walt Whitman wrote these poems on the Civil War after serving
as a war nurse in Washington.
His innovative free verse, fresh symbolism, intuitional
or transcendental views, and beliefs in the individual, are
but some the important reasons for his continuing popularity.
Some consider "When Lilacs Last in the Dooryard Bloom'd"
the best poem ever written about President Lincoln.

Walt Whitman's verses on war (and other subjects) are standard high school and college reading.

346. Whittier, John Greenleaf. "Barbara Frietchie." IN WAR TIME, 1864; rpt. pp. 190-191, THE GOLDEN TREASURY OF POETRY. Illustrated by Joan Walsh Anglund. Edited by Louis Untermeyer. New York: Golden Press, 1959, 324 pp. (all ages).

Barbara Frietchie presents a strong willed woman living amidst the Confederate soldiers who refuses to remove her Union flag.

347. Wibberly, Leonard. THE MOUSE THAT ROARED. New York: Little, Brown, 1955, 279 pp. (ages 12-adult).

Leonard Wibberly (also writing under the pseudonyms of Patrick O'Connor, Leonard Holton, and Christopher Webb) is a respected, prolific writer of books for both children and adults. THE MOUSE THAT ROARED (perhaps because it was made into a movie) is his best known. It is a humorous account of a fictional, tiny country that manages to get control of a weapon (an atomic bomb) that can destroy an entire continent with the push of one button.
The humorous approach to what is in reality a very serious possibility make for an uneasy book, part of a "mouse" series of books.
Another important series he wrote is more serious. It is a four-part biography of Thomas Jefferson: YOUNG MAN FROM THE PIEDMONT: THE YOUTH OF THOMAS JEFFERSON, 1963, 184 pp.; A DAWN IN THE TREES: THOMAS JEFFERSON, THE YEARS 1776 TO 1789, 1964, 188 pp.; THE GALES OF SPRING: THOMAS JEFFERSON, THE YEARS 1789-1801, 1965, 180 pp.; and THE TIME OF THE HARVEST: THOMAS JEFFERSON, THE YEARS 1801 TO 1826, 1966, 170 pp.; all of them published by Farrar Straus, and collected in one volume in 1968 under the title MAN OF LIBERTY: A LIFE OF THOMAS JEFFERSON.
These are written in what Leonard Wibberley calls an attempt at non-fiction/fiction (a confusing term that seems to mean something on the nature of a combination of thorough re-search and invented dialogue--containing both the facts and an attempt to humanize the characters).
Among his many other books is the seven part Treegate series about a family that lives during the Revolutionary War and the Battle of 1812, a highly complementary biography, THE LIFE OF WINSTON CHURCHILL, 1956, and a novel about a Confed-erate soldier who attempts to recover both physically and spiritually following the Civil War, THE WOUND OF PETER WAYNE (New York: Farrar, Straus, 1955, 220 pp.)

348. Williams, Jay. JOAN OF ARC. Consultant, Charles Wayland Lightboy. New York: American Heritage, 1963, 153 pp. (ages 12-adult).

This is an excellent history of Joan of Arc, attempting to present her from as impartial a viewpoint as possible. It contains many illustrations connected with her throughout history and a brief "Further Reference" section.

As the book points out, whether or not she was truly a saint, "one thing is certain: Joan was an extraordinary person, possibly a genius."

349. Wisler, G. Clifton. THUNDER ON THE TENNESSEE. New York: Dutton, 1983, 192 pp. (ages 10-16).

Sixteen-year-old Willie Delamer, a Confederate infantryman, awaits the next day's encounter with the Union soldiers at Pittsburg Landing. From this opening scene, the novel then flashes back to trace the events that brought Willie to where he is.

This is a blunt, realistic portrayal of war (vividly recreating scenes of Shiloh), focusing on a young boy who, contrary to most such characters, is not innocent, but, rather, has a bit of knowledge about war--his father is a veteran--and has a good deal of intelligence. Nevertheless, when he faces the reality, he learns it is even worse than he suspected; yet he still believes that one must face one's duty.

The father-son relationship is the well told center of the novel. It won the Golden Spur Award for Best Western Juvenile Book.

Two sequels were written: THE TRIDENT BRAND (New York: Doubleday, 1982), in which Willie returns home from the war to face a violent brother; and BUFFALO MOON (Lobestar, 1984), which traces Willie's experience living with Comanches before his experiences in the Civil War.

Among his other books, Wisler has also written CRY OF ANGRY THUNDER (New York: Doubleday, 1980), a book about Johnny Whitelock and an Indian named Antelope Foot, who grew up together but later became enemies in the battles of Black Kettle, Sand Creek, and The Little Big Horn.

350. Wondriska, William. JOHN JOHN TWILLIGER. Illustrated by the author. New York: Holt, Rinehart and Winston, 1966, 38 pp. (ages 4-7).

This wonderfully illustrated book on modulating gray pages in black-and-red tells the tale of Machine-Gun Man, who rules the town of Merryall from a Fort on top of a big hill. No one is allowed to do much of anything, including being friends with anyone else. However, John John Twilliger is a mischief maker and continually breaks the rules. One day, while dancing with Fred the Dog in a cave--dogs are not allowed in Merryall--John John ends up following Fred straight up the big hill and into the fort of the Machine-Gun Man. As it turns out, the Machine-Gun Man had covered his head and become so mean because he was afraid that people would tease him about his red hair. When John John points out the obvious, that he and Fred also have red hair and are not teased, the Machine-Gun Man discards his armor and weapons and rules the town in a friendly manner.

The story and conclusion follow a common pattern, but the characters and the language and illustrations are all fresh. It is a good book for younger children.

351. Wondriska, William. THE TOMATO PATCH. Illustrated by the author. New York: Holt, 1964. (ages 5-8).

Krullerberg and Appletainia begin by putting all their resources into weapon making, but later discover the joys of agriculture and beat their swords into plowshares. This is a satire on the cold war by an excellent illustrator.

352. Woolson, Constance Fenimore. "Kentucky Belle"; rpt. pp. 192-195, THE GOLDEN TREASURY OF POETRY. New York: Golden Press, 1959, 324 pp. (all ages).

The heroine of the poem has divided loyalties, but mainly is drawn to help a fellow human in suffering.

353. Wyndham, Joan. LOVE LESSONS; A WARTIME DIARY. New York: Little, Brown, 1985, 203 pp. (14-adult).

These memoirs of Joan Wyndham at seventeen years old begin with her coming of age among the artists of London's Chelsea district, but turn dark as the bombs begin to fall.

354. Yolen, Jane. THE MINSTREL AND THE MOUNTAIN: A TALE OF PEACE. Illustrated by Anne Rockwell. New York: World Publishing Company, 1967, 60 pp. (ages 4-8).

This is a simple parable about two kingdoms who are jealous of each other and vow to go to war. A minstrel promises each the wealth of the other. They each leave their kingdom and march around the mountain to the other's kingdom, which has been left empty. In this way, each kingdom learns that the other kingdom is no better than its own.
The illustrations are childlike line drawings filled with color. They have a flat, cartoonish quality, which matches the style of the writing.
The book might be useful for showing children that, to use an old cliche, the grass is not always greener on the other side of the hill.

355. Young, Margaret B. THE PICTURE LIFE OF MARTIN LUTHER KING, JR. New York: Franklin Watts, 1968, 45 pp. (ages 5-8).

This photobiography of a great man of peace presents the basic facts and beliefs in simple prose and black-and-white photographs. It is meant for young children.

356. Zolotow, Charlotte. THE HATING BOOK. Illustrated by Ben Shecter. New York: Harper and Row, 32 pp. (ages 4-8).

A young girl misunderstands what her friend says, and for a short period of time, until the misunderstanding is cleared up, the friendship is dissolved. During this time, the girl's mother continually tells her to ask the friend directly what the problem is. When the girl finally takes her mother's advice, the misunderstanding is cleared up.
While the book does not deal directly with war, it is a

good model for resolving conflict.

357.   Zolotow, Charlotte. THE QUARRELING BOOK. Illustrated by
Arnold Lobel. New York: Harper and Row, 1963, 28 pp. (ages
4-8).

     Mr. James forgot to tell Mrs. James good-bye. This made
her cross, and started a chain reaction. A friendly action
later reverses the process.

358.   Zyskind, Sara. STOLEN YEARS. Translated by Marganit
Inbav. New York: Signet, 1983, 232 pp. (ages 14-adult).

     This is the autobiography of Sara Plager Zyskind, a Jew,
who was eleven when the Nazis invaded Poland, seventeen when
their reign of terror ended. She suffered from typhoid, but
survived Auschwitz through an intuitive decision to cross from
the group she was in (which she later realized was being led
to the gas chambers) to a group passing by because she
recognized a former acquaintance--for some reason, no one
caught her making the switch)--also surviving the Mottelstein
Labor Camp, she finally reached the promised land, Israel,
only to face the Israel-Arab wars that began in 1948.
     STOLEN YEARS is a hard hitting story of a young girl's
odyssey from innocence through the horror of the Nazi
concentration camps to a mature, though far from ideal,
adulthood. It is a well written account of the terrible acts
humans are capable of, a story of human survival beneath the
wheels of organized brutality.

REFERENCES FOR ADULTS

359. Austill, Chris and Shelley Berman and Susan Jones, ed.
MAKING HISTORY: A SOCIAL STUDIES CURRICULUM. Cambridge, Mass.:
Educators for Social Responsibility, 1984, 90 pp.

This book is one of five short curriculum guides
resulting from the coming together of a group of teachers
concerned with the issues of growing up in the nuclear age
(refer to TAKING PART: AN ELEMENTARY CURRICULUM for more
information on the over-all set-up).
MAKING HISTORY: A SOCIAL STUDIES CURRICULUM takes as its
theme the idea "that students can and should be given
opportunities to take part in the significant events in their
world." Teachers, then, should create opportunities for
students to experience the possibilities for participation, to
understand the process of group decision making and the
political process, and to experience their potential for
making a real difference in the world.
Among the other activities, students are asked to choose
an issue that they feel should be addressed, research it, and
implement it.

360. Cloud, Kate, et al. WATERMELONS NOT WAR: A SUPPORT BOOK
FOR PARENTING IN THE NUCLEAR AGE. Philadelphia, PA: New
Society Publishers, 1984, 163 pp.

Though it is already a bit dated, WATERMELONS NOT WAR: A
SUPPORT BOOK FOR PARENTING IN THE NUCLEAR AGE is one of the
better books for helping adults introduce the subject of
nuclear war to children. It was put together by the Nuclear
Education Project (five women who came together as a group
after the Three Mile Island accident--Kate Cloud, Alice Evans,
Ellie Deegan, Hayat Imam, and Barbara Signer). Its subject
matter extends beyond nuclear war to nuclear power of all
forms, and it explains in easily understood terms how nuclear
energy works.
More importantly, it deals with the realities of living
in a nuclear age and how children can be exposed to these
realities without being plunged into a state of despair; in
fact, the main thrust of the book is to show children positive
activities to help prevent the negative possibilities. A
number of poems, drawings, and statements from children are
included. Lists of organizations and resources (dated)
working for peace and a better understanding of atomic energy
are included, as are lists of books for children and for
adults that deal with peace (i.e., THE STORY OF FERDINAND) and

war (i.e., THE PUSHCART WAR).
     A letter by Dr. Helen Caldicott praising the book is
included as an "Afterword." It begins:

          WATERMELONS NOT WAR reiterates the need for every
          parent to face the nuclear weapons dilemma. But
          we don't have much time. The children know it . . .

361. Condon, Camy and James McGinnis. PUPPETS FOR PEACE. St.
Louis, MO: The Institute for Peace and Justice, 1984, 44 pp.

     This book has a guidebook, instructions, and scripts for
participatory puppetry on conflict resolution and peace making. It is a valuable guide for conducting peace learning
activities at schools, churches, and other community organizations. Each unit contains a brief bibliography of related
books.

362. Dorn, Lois and Penni Eldredge-Martin. PEACE IN THE
FAMILY: A WORKBOOK OF IDEAS & ACTIONS. New York: Pantheon
Books, 1983, 177 pp.

     This book, a successor to A MANUAL ON NONVIOLENCE AND
CHILDREN, is the result of the Nonviolence and Children
Program's Parent Support Project and is meant to encourage
people to nurture children in an atmosphere of support and
affirmation. In practical terms, the purpose of the book is
to help readers set up ways for sorting out, gaining feedback
on, and evaluating personal attitudes about building relationships, especially relationships between adults and children.
It offers a wide range of exercises, practical programs, and
examples for the purpose of establishing two-way communica-
tions between generations.
     It contains an annotated bibliography of "hands-on books
found readable, stimulating, and encouraging" on building relationships.
     This is a good book for the average reader interested in
getting more involved with non-violence.

363. Dougall, Lucy, ed. WAR AND PEACE IN LITERATURE: PROSE,
DRAMA AND POETRY WHICH ILLUMINATE THE PROBLEM OF WAR. Chicago:
World Without War Publications, 1982, 171 pp.

     This is an excellent annotated listing of novels and
plays which, as Robert Pickus states in the introduction,
"hold a mirror up to war, revealing the ways in which it
enhances and even ennobles, as well as destroys and degrades,
those subject to its demands. It also includes selections of
poetry and listings of reference works, criticism, anthologies
and essays on the subject.

364. Dowling, John. WAR. PEACE. FILM GUIDE., rev. ed.,
Chicago: World Without War Publications, 1980, 188 pp.

     This excellent annotated guide to films dealing with war
and peace includes suggestions about using the films in the

classroom, lists supplementary reading material, and includes
a detailed guide to further resources.
     The films are listed by subject (including a grouping of
"Children's Films"), as well as alphabetically.

365. Foster, Julian and Durward Long, eds. PROTEST: STUDENT
ACTIVISM IN AMERICA. New York: William Morrow, 1970, 596 pp.

     This thick book attempts to offer an objective overview
of the student protests taking place in America during the
Vietnam War. It is divided up into five parts: 1. The Con-
flict--overviews of activism; 2. The Activists--backgrounds
and personalities of some of the more well known activists; 3.
Scenes of Conflict: Seven Case Studies; 4. New Patterns of
Power--attempts to generalize; and 5. Perspectives on Pro-
test--views and interpretations.
     The book seems to be a sincere attempt, though its
interest today might be more from a looking-back at the
happenings of the time than anything else.

366. Gould, Benina Berger and Susan Moon and Judith Van
Hoorn, ed. GROWING UP SCARED?: THE PSYCHOLOGICAL EFFECTS OF
THE NUCLEAR THREAT ON CHILDREN. California: Open Books, 1986,
224 pp.

     This book, based on the Nuclear Ecology Research Con-
ference, 1986, offers sixteen articles by educators, research
psychologists and clinicians, and a transcript of a youth
panel, where eleven youth speak about growing up under the
threat of nuclear war--all of the articles (except the youth
panel) edited or rewritten following their presentation at the
conference. Some black-and-white photographs of the children
on the panel are also included.
     The book deals with the implications of how we understand
the hopes and fears of young people today under the threat of
immediate annihilation and offers numerous perspectives for
working with them in maintaining mental health.
     An appendix, "A Review of the Literature," offers the
findings of various research addressing questions of the consequences of children growing up in a time of fear and un-
certainty caused by the nuclear arms race. It is aimed at a
scholarly approach to the problem.

367. Gregory, Donna, ed. THE NUCLEAR PREDICAMENT: A
SOURCEBOOK. New York: St. Martin's Press, 1986, 403 pp.

     This book is the result of a three year class experience
at UCLA, where the subject of nuclear war was introduced to a
freshman English course and a university-wide interdiscipli-
nary course. It provides a vast amount of material on nuclear
war, and can serve as a good introduction to the subject for
older children and adults.

368. Greiner, Rosmarie. PEACE EDUCATION: A BIBLIOGRAPHY
FOCUSING ON YOUNG CHILDREN. Santa Cruz, CA: Peace
Education/Eschaton Foundation, 1983, 20 pp.

Rosmarie Greiner, basing the need for such a book on the
belief that "attitudes and values have their beginnings in
early childhood" and "books are very much a part of this early
socialization process," has put together an annotated bibliography grouped around six components of peace education: 1)
self awareness; 2) awareness of others; 3) conflict resolution; 4) love of nature; 5) global awareness; and 6) imagination. There is also an appendix of books for children ages
6-12 and one for adults.
     The component on conflict resolution has a list of thirty
books and is the most central to the subject of war and peace.
It is a brief bibliography with brief annotations--a worthwhile place to begin.

369. Haessly, Jacqueline. PEACEMAKING: FAMILY ACTIVITIES FOR
JUSTICE AND PEACE. New York: Paulist Press, 1980, 86 pp.

     Jacqueline Haessly, the coordinator of the Milwaukee
Peace Education Center, has put together a collection of
practical, philosophical, and spiritual information and
insight to help the family work together for peace.
     The book is divided into two parts: "Steppingstones to
Pease," and "Families in a Global Village." Part I offers
suggestions for four areas of development: affirmation, respect for differences, cooperation, and creative resolution
of conflict. Part 2 expands the focus from the family to the
"global society," closing with a celebration of the global
village.
     It is part of the Family Enrichment Materials in the
Paths of Life Family Life Program and expresses a strong
Christian viewpoint.

370. Judson, Stephanie, ed. A MANUAL ON NONVIOLENCE AND
CHILDREN. Philadelphia, PA: New Society Publishers, 1977, 152
pp.

     This excellent manual is an outgrowth of the work of the
Nonviolence and Children Program begun in 1969 by the Friends
of Peace Committee in Philadelphia, especially during the
years 1973-1976, and is based on the program's experiences in
schools, with parents, teachers, and international groups.
Based on the idea that adults have the responsibility to
inspire in children the desire and ability to resolve conflicts without the use of violence, it offers teachers con-
crete ideas for creating an atmosphere where children can gain
skills in conflict resolution and develop the thinking and
behavior necessary for peaceful living in the contemporary
world.

371. Keyes, Jr., Ken. THE HUNDREDTH MONKEY. 2nd ed., Coos
Bay, Oregon: Vision Books, 1986, 176 pp.

     Ken Keyes, Jr., states that this book is the result of
two events, his viewing of THE LAST EPIDEMIC, a video-tape of
scientists and physicians at a symposium discussing the unac-
ceptability of nuclear weapons for human health, and his ex-
posure to the Hundredth Monkey Phenomenon, which in parable
form says that "when a certain critical number achieves an

awareness, this new awareness may be communicated from mind to mind." In other words, once a certain number of people become aware of the dangers of nuclear arms build-up, this awareness will suddenly spread through the entire world and there will be a swing away from the stockpiling of such weapons,

In order to spread the word, the book is not copyrighted, and readers are encouraged to reproduce it, or parts of it.

It is a collection of facts (i.e., "The failure of a 46 cent computer part has produced a false signal that Russian missiles were on the way."), statements by knowledgeable people (i.e., "'Nuclear weapons aren't weapons--they're an obscenity,' said Dr. Marvin Goldberger, President, California Institute of Technology."), and "words of wisdom": "However much our ideas and ideologies may clash, we must remember that nothing is more important for survival and for happiness in life than feelings of understanding and commonness of human purpose."

372. Klubock, Dorothy, ed. TAKING PART: AN ELEMENTARY CURRICULUM. Cambridge, Mass.: Educators for Social Responsibility, 1984, 53 pp.

This book is the result of the coming together of a group of teachers in 1981 to discuss the issue of growing up in a nuclear age, resulting in the formation of the Educators for Social Responsibility, "whose goal is to provide materials, education, and support for teachers and students in dealing with this issue."

What the group found in subsequent research was that students, as they grew older, gained a sense of powerlessness and cynicism. Determined to find a response to the growing apathy, the group began brainstorming a curriculum on participation. This book is one of five short curriculum guides developed for what the group calls the "Participation Series."

They state that the book's purpose is twofold: one, to lay a "foundation in participation for elementary school children," and two, to "provide the children we teach with an age-appropriate understanding of the process of political elections."

They stress the term "empowerment" as very important to the purpose of the book, denoting the "positive effect on children of discovering their self-worth, their ability to make meaningful decisions, and their potential to act and to make things happen in their lives."

Another book in the series, MAKING HISTORY, also applies to the subject of war and peace.

373. Lemoine, Julie and Randi Farkas. LET'S TALK ABOUT PEACE; LET'S TALK ABOUT NUCLEAR WAR: A PEACE CURRICULUM FOR TEACHING IN THE NUCLEAR AGE. Illustrated by Jeannie Dodha. Unit VII originated and illustrated by Susan Dembowski. 150 pp.

The authors "want to aid and encourage you and the children in your care to speak openly about the subject of nuclear war." To accomplish this, they have put together ways of introducing a peace curriculum at school, including such items as a "Sample Letter to Parents," a "Curriculum Purpose" statement, a superintendent's views for teaching about nuclear

issues, and several survey formats. In addition, there are
seven units: "Expressing Thoughts and Feelings"; "What Makes
an Enemy"; "Peace as a Process"; "History of Nonviolence";
"War and Nuclear Facts"; "Survival of the Cooperative"; "
Action and Empowerment."
     The book contains many practical ideas for introducing
conflict and conflict resolution to elementary students.

374. Lifton, Robert J. and Nicholas Humphrey, ed. IN A DARK
TIME: IMAGES FOR SURVIVAL. Mass.: Harvard University Press,
1984, 154 pp.

     This is an excellent anthology of the thoughts and
writings of a vast array of people from the past 2500
years--Sappho, Robert Lowell, Saint John the Divine, Martin
Luther King, Jr., Seneca, Winston Churchill, a Hiroshima
grocer, a Turkish dissident, soldiers, churchmen, statesmen,
writers, government leaders.
     As the authors state, these thoughts and writings are
"about the psychological and imaginative confusion that surrounds popular ideas of war--of valor, victory over enemies,
and death . . . . It is designed, quite deliberately, as an
emetic against war." And it is effective, both emotionally
and logically persuasive.

375. Lifton, Robert J. and Richard Falk. INDEFENSIBLE
WEAPONS: THE POLITICAL AND PSYCHOLOGICAL CASE AGAINST
NUCLEARISM. New York: Basic Books, 1982, 301 pp.

     This book explores the changing attitudes toward nuclear
weapons since the early 1980s. It defines nuclearism as
psychological, political, and military dependence on nuclear
weapons, in specific, the embracement of nuclear weapons as a
solution to a variety of human dilemmas (most ironically,
"security").
     Lifton examines the psychological impact, what he calls
the struggle to "imagine the real," and Falk examines the
political and tactical issues, i.e., the "anatomy of nuclearism."

376. Meier, Paulette and Beth McPherson. NUCLEAR DANGERS: A
RESOURCE GUIDE FOR SECONDARY SCHOOL TEACHERS. Washington,
D.C.: The Nuclear Information and Resource Service, 1983, 28
pp.

     This is an excellent, though already dated, annotated
bibliography of articles and books on nuclear issues put
together as a response to requests from hundreds of educators,
who wrote "to NIRS in search of educational materials which
present a critical examination of the nuclear weapons and
nuclear power issues."

377. Peachey, J. Lorne. HOW TO TEACH PEACE TO CHILDREN.
Scottdale, PA: Herald Press, 1981, 32 pp.

     J. Lorne Peachey, editor of CHRISTIAN LIVING, published
by the Mennonite Publishing House, has put together a "prac-

tical resource for parents and families who don't want to just
mouth peace language, but desire to find practical handles to
build peacemaking lifestyles in the home and community" as
part of his involvement with the New Call to Peacemaking
(NCP), which began in 1975 as "a historic peace church effort
to rediscover and reaffirm the biblical base and Christ-cen-
teredness for a peace witness."

After a brief introduction explaining the book's purpose,
there are four short chapters: "The Family's Responsibility
for Teaching Peace," Twenty Suggestions for Teaching Peace to
Children in the Home," "The Church Meeting and the Home Working Together," and "Suggestions for Guiding Group Discussions." A brief bibliography is included.

This is a good short introduction to dealing with issues
of peace in the family or in a small group setting. The religious overtones are obvious and may be irritating for non-
members.

378. PERSPECTIVES: A TEACHING GUIDE TO CONCEPTS OF PEACE.
(anon). Cambridge, Mass.: Educators for Social Responsibility,
1983, 402 pp.

The book attempts to "create a dialogue around the
questions of what peace means, how it can be preserved, and
who can be considered a peacemaker." It is meant to "help
teachers discuss with students the experience of personal,
social and international peace, and the structures by which
peace is promoted and preserved." It is meant as a source
book rather than a course in itself. And it includes a
valuable chapter on peacemakers.

The back cover contains the following statement about the
writers and publishers of the text:

> EDUCATORS FOR SOCIAL RESPONSIBILITY is a national,
> non-profit membership organization of educators,
> parents, and concerned individuals who believe
> that the nuclear age demands new approaches to
> education. ESR is committed to presenting diver-
> gent views in the classroom on nuclear issues,
> war, and peace; to dealing with young people's
> questions and fears about the threat of nuclear
> war; and to fostering citizen participation in
> decision-making about the nuclear arms race. ESR
> researches students' attitudes toward nuclear
> issues, assesses educational materials, develops
> curricula, sponsors conferences and professional
> development programs, and provides speakers and
> consultation services.

The book is divided into activities for K-6 and for 7-12
and includes a bibliography of resources. It is an excellent
guide for exploring issues of peace.

379. Pomainville, Martha and Cynthia Blankenship and Barbara
Stanford. CONFLICT RESOLUTION MODULES FOR HIGH SCHOOL
STUDENTS. New York: Bantam Books, 1977, 21 pp.

This is a learning structure for self-directed small
groups containing ten lessons on conflict and conflict

resolution. It is a good concise syllabus style framework for setting up and leading a discussion group on the subject.

380. Prutzman, Priscilla and M. Leonard Burger and Gretchen Bodenhamer and Lee Stern. THE FRIENDLY CLASSROOM FOR A SMALL PLANET: A HANDBOOK ON CREATIVE APPROACHES TO LIVING AND PROBLEM SOLVING FOR CHILDREN. Illustrated by Barbara Wilks and Paul Peabody. Wayne, New Jersey: Avery, 1978, 110 pp.

Containing ideas for teaching cooperation, communication, affirmation, and conflict resolution skills, and including songs, poems, and basic line drawings, this book offers many ideas for introducing cooperation and conflict resolution in the classroom.
It has a bibliography of additional books on conflict and conflict resolution.

381. Riordan, Michael, ed. THE DAY AFTER MIDNIGHT: THE EFFECTS OF NUCLEAR WAR. Palo Alto, California: Cheshire Books, 1982, 143 pp.

Based on a report, "The Effects of Nuclear War," published in 1979 by the Office of Technology Assessment (OTA), United States Congress, the book examines four plausible nuclear attack scenarios (from single weapon detonation results to all out war), reaching the conclusion that "in all cases a nuclear war would be an unmitigated catastrophe."
The premise of the book is "that people should be well informed about this highly controversial issue so they can make appropriate decisions. . . . Such an informed public, it is hoped, should be able to make better decisions about the use and disposal of nuclear weapons."
Though dated in some ways, as any such book becomes almost immediately in the ever changing development of nuclear weapons, the book nevertheless presents highly knowledgeable scenarios on likely occurrences if nuclear war should happen, and the likely scenarios really have not changed greatly since the book's publication.
This is a useful introduction to the nuclear world we live in. It is illustrated with charts and maps, contains a glossary of nuclear jargon, and has a list of reference books.

382. SOVIET MILITARY POWER: 1986. Washington, D.C.: U.S. Government, 1986, 156 pp.

Each year (since 1981), the United States Department of Defense has put out this book, which offers detailed statistics of exactly what the title claims. It also contains a strong push to keep U.S. military power strong in order to maintain the balance of power (or, rather, to get the U.S. power up to that of the Soviet Union).
It is a good source of statistics, but slanted, and should be read with some other source outside of the government, such as THE DAY AFTER MIDNIGHT: THE EFFECTS OF NUCLEAR WAR, edited by Michael Riordan.

383.   Van Ornum, William and Mary Wicker Van Ornum. TALKING
TO CHILDREN ABOUT NUCLEAR WAR. New York: Continuum, 1984, 99
pp.

     The authors, a clinical psychologist and a journalist
specializing in educational materials for young people, draw
on the expertise of numerous professionals and leaders, from
Betty Bumpers to Robert J. Lifton, in the dialogue about nuclear war.   Basing their justification for the book on the
fact that potential nuclear holocaust is a fact of life that
will not disappear by ignoring it and that children hear about
it and encounter it constantly (in video games, in television
shows, in movies, and in the music they listen to), the authors have attempted to put together a book that focuses on
"the FEELINGS this topic evokes." It is not an attempt to
offer a political stance, to debate the morality of the subject, to include analytical or ideological discussions, or to
suggest additional reading materials.   Instead, it offers a
"psychological examination of the human emotions and religious
responses evoked by talk of nuclear war."
     The book is meant to be a guide for beginning a needed
dialogue between adults and children about the topic and does
serve to lay out the general boundaries.

384.   White, Bishop C. Dale, ed. IN DEFENSE OF CREATION: THE
NUCLEAR CRISIS AND A JUST PEACE: THE FOUNDATION DOCUMENT OF
THE UNITED METHODIST COUNCIL OF BISHOPS. Tennessee: Graded
Press, 1986, 96 pp.

     This is the official position of the Methodist Church on
peace and war, particularly nuclear war, offering the heritage
of peace within the Methodist Church, various possible posi-
tions on war and peace, policies for a Just Peace, and other
discussions about the current nuclear arms race.
     It is, obviously, a religious perspective, and yet a
liberal one.

385.   Wyden, Peter. DAY ONE: BEFORE HIROSHIMA AND AFTER. New
York: Simon and Schuster, 1984, 412 pp.

     This is a detailed, in depth history of the development
of the Atom Bomb, its use on Hiroshima, and subsequent devel-
opments.
     It contains many black-and-white photographs and maps on
the inside covers of Hiroshima and the bomb's area of destruction.
     This is an excellent source for the facts behind this
dramatic event.

386.   Young, David S., ed. STUDY WAR NO MORE: A PEACE HANDBOOK
FOR YOUTH. Elgin, Ill.: Brethren Press, 1981, 95 pp.

     David S. Young, a pastor in the Church of the Brethren,
has prepared this book for use with a teen-age audience. It
contains eight study chapters, each with questions and answers.
     Obviously, a Christian perspective, the final chapter,
"The Shalom Community," ends:

We shall know Christ by the new community, the
Shalom Community, in which we are all called to
share.   That community extends around the world
with differences as large as the human heart, but
none so great that they can't fit into the hand of
God.   Peacemaking with the person next door leads
to peacemaking around the world.   Peacemaking begins at home and heads to the throne of God.

As is often the case with church related publications,
the religious beliefs sometimes interfere with the subjects of
peace and war.   Nevertheless, it is true that many of these
same churches are among the leading groups working for peace
in today's world.

Index

[Numbers indicate entry numbers.]

About the Compiler

HARRY EDWIN EISS is Assistant Professor of English at Eastern Michigan University, Ypsilanti, Michigan. He is the author of *Dictionary of Language Games, Puzzles, and Amusements* (Greenwood Press, 1986) and *Dictionary of Mathematical Games, Puzzles, and Amusements* (Greenwood Press, 1988). He has also published articles on language arts instruction, and his poems have appeared in several anthologies. His critiques of the works of Janet Lunn and Monica Hughes will appear in *Beacham's Guide to Literature for Young Adults* (forthcoming). He has also participated in a National Endowment for the Arts seminar with his presentation "Children's Classics: The Victorian Age."